ROUGH
GUIDES

POCKET **ROUGH GUIDE**
LAS VEGAS

CONTENTS

LAS VEGAS

A dazzling oasis where about forty million people a year escape the everyday, Las Vegas has made a fine art of indulging its visitors' every appetite. From its ever-changing architecture to cascading chocolate fountains, adrenaline-pumping zip lines and jaw-dropping stage shows, everything is built to thrill; as soon as the novelty wears off, it's blown up and replaced with something bigger and better. The city of excess is home to many of the largest hotels in the world – and that's pretty much all – but it's these extraordinary creations everyone comes to see.

Fremont Street Experience

Best places to get a view of the Strip

Although towering hotel blocks jostle for position along the Strip, there are surprisingly few places that offer non-guests a panoramic view of the whole thing. Possibilities include the summit of the Stratosphere (but that's a little far north and not quite aligned with the Strip), and the Voodoo Rooftop Nightclub at the Rio, off to one side. So the winner is – the observation platform at the top of Paris's Eiffel Tower (see page 49), perfectly poised to look north and south along the Strip's busiest stretch, as well as west, and down, to the fountains of Bellagio.

Each hotel is a neighbourhood in its own right, measuring as much as a mile end to end; crammed full of state-of-the-art clubs, restaurants, spas and pools; and centring on what makes the whole thing possible – an action-packed casino where tourists and tycoons alike are gripped by the roll of the dice and the turn of the card.

Even if its entire urban area covers 136 square miles, most visitors see no more of Las Vegas than two short, and very different, linear stretches. Downtown, the original centre, now amounts to four brief (roofed-over) blocks of Fremont Street, while the Strip begins a couple of miles south, just beyond the city limits, and runs for four miles southwest. It's the Strip where the real action is, a visual feast where each mega-casino vies to outdo the next with some outlandish theme, be it an Egyptian pyramid (*Luxor*), a Roman extravaganza (*Caesars Palace*), a fairytale castle (*Excalibur*) or a European city (*Paris* and the *Venetian*).

In 1940, Las Vegas was home to just eight thousand people. It owes its extraordinary growth to its constant willingness to adapt; far from remaining kitsch and old-fashioned, it's forever reinventing itself. Entrepreneurs race to spot the latest shift in who has the money and what they want to spend it on. A few years ago the casinos realized that gamblers were happy to pay premium prices for good food, and top chefs now run gourmet restaurants in venues like *Bellagio* and the *Cosmopolitan*. More recently, demand from younger visitors has prompted casinos like *Wynn Las Vegas* and *MGM Grand* to open high-tech nightclubs to match those of Miami and LA.

The reputation Las Vegas still enjoys, of being a quasi-legal adult playground where (almost) anything goes, dates back to its early years when most of its first generation of luxury resorts were cut-throat rivals controlled by the Mob. In those days illegal profits could easily be "skimmed" off and respectable investors steered clear. Then, as now, visitors loved to imagine that they were rubbing shoulders with gangsters. Standing well back from the Strip, each casino was a labyrinth in which it was all but impossible to find an exit. During the 1980s, however, visitors started to explore on foot; mogul Steve Wynn cashed in by placing a flame-spouting volcano outside his new Mirage mega-resort. As the casinos competed to lure in pedestrians, they filled in the daunting distances from the sidewalk, and between casinos.

With Las Vegas booming in the 1990s, gaming corporations bought up first individual casinos, and then each other. The Strip today is dominated by just two colossal conglomerates – MGM Resorts and Caesars Entertainment. Once you own the casino next

When to visit

Visitors flock to Las Vegas throughout the year, however the climate varies enormously. In July and August, the average daytime high exceeds 100°F (38°C), while in winter the thermometer regularly drops below freezing. Hotel swimming pools generally open between April and September only.
It's which day you visit that you should really take into account; accommodation can easily cost twice as much on Friday and Saturday as during the rest of the week.

door, there's no reason to make each a virtual prison; the Strip has therefore opened out, so that much of its central portion now consists of open-air terraces and pavilions housing bars and restaurants.

The city may have tamed its setting, but the magnificent

wildernesses of the American West still lie on its doorstep. Dramatic parks like Red Rock Canyon and the Valley of Fire are just a short drive away, or you can fly to the Grand Canyon, and Utah's glorious Zion National Park makes a wonderful overnight getaway.

Valley of Fire

Where to...

Shop

Shopping now ranks among the principal reasons that people visit Las Vegas. **Downtown** is all but devoid of shops, however, and while the workaday city has its fair share of malls, tourists do almost all of their shopping on **the Strip** itself. Their prime destination is the amazing **Forum** at Caesars Palace, followed by the **Grand Canal Shoppes** at the Venetian and **Miracle Mile** at Planet Hollywood. Stand-alone malls include **Fashion Show** opposite Wynn Las Vegas, useful for everyday purchases, and high-end **Crystals** in CityCenter.
OUR FAVOURITES: Town Square, see page 32. Miracle Mile Shops, see page 56. Grand Canal Shoppes, see page 70.

Eat

Las Vegas used to be a byword for bad food, with just the occasional mobster-dominated steakhouse or Italian restaurant to relieve the monotony of the pile-'em-high **buffets**. Those days have long gone. Every major **Strip casino** now holds half a dozen or more high-quality restaurants, many run by top chefs from all over the world. Prices have soared, to a typical minimum spend of $50 per head at big-name places, but so too have standards, and you could eat a great meal in a different restaurant every night in casinos such as Aria, Bellagio, Caesars Palace, the Cosmopolitan and the Venetian.
OUR FAVOURITES: The Buffet at Aria, see page 44. Beijing Noodle No. 9, Caesars, see page 57. Bouchon at the Venetian, see page 71.

Drink

Every Las Vegas casino offers free drinks to gamblers. Sit at a slot machine or gaming table, and a cocktail waiter will find you and take your order (tips are expected). In addition, the casinos feature all kinds of bars and lounges. Along the Strip, bars tend to be themed, as with the Irish pubs of **New York–New York** or the flamboyant lounges of **Caesars Palace**; downtown they're a bit more rough-and-ready. Note that the legal drinking age is 21 – you must carry ID to prove it.
OUR FAVOURITES: Cleopatra's Barge, see page 59. Downtown Cocktail Room, see page 85. Double Down Saloon, see page 94.

Go out

The Strip is once more riding high as the entertainment epicentre of the world. While Elvis may have left the building, headliners like **David Copperfield** and **Celine Dion** attract thousands of big-spending fans night after night. Meanwhile the old-style feathers-and-sequins revues have been supplanted by a stream of lavish shows by **Cirque du Soleil** and the likes of the postmodern **Blue Man Group**. A new generation of visitors has been responsible for the dramatic growth in the city's clubbing scene. Casinos like the **Cosmopolitan**, the **Palms** and **Wynn Las Vegas** now boast some of the world's most spectacular – and expensive – nightclubs and ultra-lounges.
OUR FAVOURITES: Light, see page 36. Human Nature, see page 76. Terry Fator, see page 76.

Las Vegas at a glance

The rest of the city p.86.
Real people live real lives in Las Vegas's
outlying residential districts, but for visitors
the major landmarks are yet more casinos,
with standouts including the Rio, the Palms
and the Hard Rock.

The North Strip p.62.
Two deadly rival mega-complexes, the Venetian/Palazzo
and Wynn Las Vegas/Encore lock horns at the northern
end of the Strip. The area beyond them to the north was
hit hard by recession, with veteran casinos vanishing and
new developments abandoned incomplete.

CityCenter and around p.38.
The Strip's first separate "neighbourhood",
unveiled by MGM Resorts in 2009 and
centring on the modernist Aria, also includes
Bellagio, as well as an unwanted interloper,
the Cosmopolitan.

The South Strip p.24.
With their playful architecture and
varied attractions, the high-profile,
MGM-owned casinos at the southern
end of the Strip – Mandalay Bay,
Luxor, Excalibur, New York–New York
and the MGM Grand – are hugely
popular with younger visitors.

Downtown Las Vegas p.78.
The few blocks where it all began have bounced back in recent years, with the unique Fremont Street Experience and the Mob Museum drawing the crowds.

N

The Central Strip p.48.
The long-standing heart of the Strip, which includes veterans like the Flamingo and Caesars Palace as well as the newer Paris, belongs entirely to Caesars Entertainment, and has become its most pedestrian-friendly segment.

▷ **The deserts** p.96.
For a taste of Nevada's desert scenery, venture twenty miles west of Las Vegas to Red Rock Canyon. Wonders further afield include Arizona's Grand Canyon and Utah's Zion Canyon.

| 0 | kilometres | 2 |
| 0 | mile | 1 |

15

Things not to miss

It's not possible to see everything that Las Vegas has to offer in one trip – and we don't suggest you try. What follows is a selective taste of the highlights, from its most opulent casinos to the dramatic scenery of the deserts.

> The Forum Shops
See page 56
America's most profitable shopping mall, stuffed inside the faux-Roman pomp of Caesars Palace – though the price tags are real enough.

< Grand Canyon South Rim
See page 100
Seeing Arizona's world-famous wonder makes a fabulous weekend road trip, but you can also fly there and back in a day.

∨ The Venetian
See page 63
Festooned with dazzling frescoes and echoing to the song of costumed gondoliers, the opulent Venetian is loved by kids, clubbers and culture vultures alike.

< Le Village Buffet
See page 57
Possibly the classiest buffet in town, serving classic French cuisine with a kitschy, Vegas twist.

∨ Bodies... The Exhibition
See page 27
What better place to look for dead bodies than a gigantic pyramid? Luxor makes an obvious home for this gruesome but uplifting exhibit.

< **Zion National Park**
See page 100
You can drive to Utah's magnificent red-rock park in little more than two hours to enjoy dramatic scenery and awe-inspiring hikes.

∨ **Dig This!**
See page 86
If you've always wanted to drive a bulldozer, or play basketball using a giant digger, this is where your dreams come true.

∧ **Kà**
See page 36
For sheer spectacle and breathtaking stunts, the most jaw-dropping Cirque show in town.

< **Stratosphere Thrill Rides**
See page 69
The craziest thrill rides of all – spin off the Stratosphere strapped to a lurching bench or simply jump off the edge.

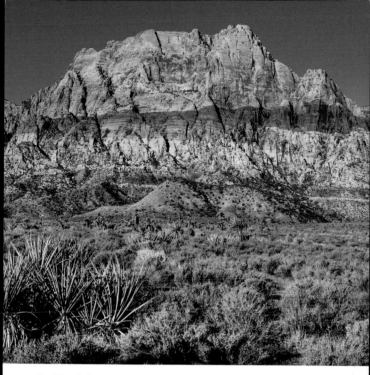

∧ **Red Rock Canyon**
See page 96
Las Vegas's great escape;
hike and bike amid stunning
sandstone peaks just twenty
miles from the Strip.

∨ **Bellagio**
See page 42
Las Vegas at its most luxurious,
an Italianate marble extravaganza
with its own eight-acre lake.

∧ The Neon Museum
See page 81
A charming, unpolished look at a Vegas icon: the neon sign. Unsurprisingly, it's most atmospheric after dark.

< Titanic: The Artifact Exhibition
See page 27
The world's only permanent display of Titanic artefacts, including a huge and very eerie chunk of the ship herself, upstairs in the Luxor pyramid.

< **Blue Man Group**
See page 36
A bizarre but compelling blend of performance art, slapstick and high-octane rock.

∨ **Hoover Dam**
See page 96
A mighty wall of concrete holding back the Colorado River – the architectural showpiece that made Las Vegas possible.

Day One in Las Vegas

 Bellagio Patisserie, Bellagio. See page 44. Head to the back of Bellagio to enjoy a morning pick-me-up of pastries, omelettes and freshly brewed coffee.

The Conservatory, Bellagio. See page 43. Part greenhouse, part camp and colourful fantasyland, Bellagio's indoor flower show must be seen to be believed.

Eiffel Tower Experience. See page 49. Ride into the skies atop Las Vegas's own miniature version of Paris and look down on the rest of the Strip.

The Conservatory, Bellagio

Lunch. See page 58. Enjoy a quintessentially French bistro meal, with a ringside seat on the Strip, at *Mon Ami Gabi* in Paris.

The Forum Shops. See page 56. Marble statues, fountains and a false sky that cycles hourly between day and night; is it ancient Rome or simply Caesars Palace?

Grand Canal Shoppes. See page 70. Operatic gondoliers ply the waters of the Grand Canal, serenading shoppers perusing the Venetian's upstairs, upmarket mall.

Entrance to The Forum Shops

Dinner. See page 73. Pan-Asian food and lush red decor at *Wazuzu* in Wynn Las Vegas combine to offer a memorable dining experience.

Love, the Mirage. See page 76. Las Vegas favourites, Cirque du Soleil, join forces with The Beatles to stunning effect.

Omnia, Caesars Palace. See page 60. Experience Las Vegas's new breed of breathtaking clubs at Caesars' showpiece indoor-outdoor *Omnia*.

Love, the Mirage

Day Two in Las Vegas

Il Fornaio, New York–New York. See page 34. This New York-style Italian bakery is the perfect place to grab breakfast.

The Big Apple Coaster, New York–New York. See page 30. Let's shake things up – loop around the Manhattan skyline in a little yellow cab, upside down, at 70mph.

Excalibur. See page 28. If things haven't been kitsch enough yet, stroll through this bizarre Arthurian castle-casino.

Luxor. See page 25. Enter an Egyptian pyramid through the paws of the Sphinx to see artefacts recovered from the Titanic.

Shark Reef, Mandalay Bay. See page 25. Watch crocodiles and sharks swim amid the ruins of a Mayan temple.

Lunch. See page 33. Break for a Mexican meal beside Mandalay Bay's wave pool, at the *Border Grill*.

CSI The Experience, MGM Grand. See page 31. Use razor-sharp forensic skills to solve a murder.

Art collection, CityCenter. See page 38. The sleek, modernist CityCenter district holds a surprising array of contemporary sculptures from the likes of Antony Gormley and Henry Moore.

The Shops at Crystals. See page 44. Las Vegas's priciest mall has a flamboyant interior that's well worth seeing.

Dinner. See page 46. Dine on superb "New Italian" food in *Scarpetta*, overlooking Bellagio's famous fountains.

Gwen Stefani. See page 61. See the global pop icon deliver a glittering song-and-dance show in the finest Las Vegas tradition.

Excalibur

Luxor

Shark Reef

Classic Las Vegas

For those who yearn for the Rat Pack-ruled Strip, corporate-owned Las Vegas can feel too tasteful for comfort. Vestiges of the old times still survive, though, if you know where to look.

Flamingo Las Vegas. See page 54. Okay, so the Flamingo these days is more Donny Osmond than Bugsy Siegel, but the original Strip resort still packs plenty of classic kitsch, including its trademark pink flamingoes.

Caesars Palace. See page 51. With its half-naked centurions and Cleopatras, Caesars is where the Strip first veered towards full-on fantasy fifty years ago – and it hasn't let up since.

Caesars Palace

Lunch. See page 83. The all-you-can-eat buffet is one tradition Las Vegas will never let go; prices have risen on the Strip, but head downtown and you'll find amazing value, at the *Paradise Buffet*, for example.

The Mob Museum. See page 81. There's no better place to learn the seedy story of Las Vegas's shady past than at this gripping, gruesome museum downtown.

El Cortez. See page 81. For the true Las Vegas experience, gamble in downtown's least-changed casino, with its hard-bitten characters and rock-bottom odds.

Dynamite at the Mob Museum

Fremont Street Experience. See page 78. All bright lights and flashing neon, downtown's must-see block-spanning canopy is pure old-fashioned spectacle.

Dinner. See page 84. *Oscar's Steakhouse*, belonging to larger-than-life former mayor Oscar Goodman, oozes unabashed love for downtown's long-lost heyday.

Peppermill Fireside Lounge. See page 74. Round things off with a martini nightcap in this flamboyant round-the-clock Stripside relic.

Fremont Street Experience

Budget Las Vegas

While Las Vegas is not the budget destination it used to be, it's still possible to visit on the cheap if you play your cards right (better still, don't play cards at all…).

Excalibur. See page 28. Wake up in your Royal Tower room at Excalibur – from $50 for a King, they're the Strip's best value.

Free monorails. See page 118. Hop on the free monorail system to see Luxor and Mandalay Bay.

The Deuce. See page 117. Ride the Deuce bus north from Mandalay Bay and enjoy the Strip in all its glory.

The Midway. See page 68. Stop off at Circus Circus to watch free circus performances on the Midway stage.

Monorail

🍽 **Lunch**. See page 56. Head for Caesars Palace and buy a "Buffet of Buffets" pass, valid for 24 hours at all Caesars' properties. Start with the *Bacchanal Buffet*, which epitomizes decadent Las Vegas excess.

Mac King. See page 61. Cross the Strip to Harrah's to enjoy the best-value show in town – the clownish, endearing Mac King and his family-fun comedy magic.

Big Elvis. See page 60. Simply stay in Harrah's and head for the no-cover Piano Bar, where the hunka-hunka love that is Pete Vallee keeps on burning all afternoon.

The Deuce

The Volcano. See page 62. Once darkness falls, take your place outside the Mirage and watch the volcano erupt.

🍽 **Dinner**. See page 57. Use your "Buffet of Buffets" pass again to sample the irresistible selection of all-French cuisine at *Le Village Buffet* in Paris.

Bellagio Fountains. See page 43. The mesmerizing jets of this free water ballet make a suitably soothing end to the day.

The Volcano

PLACES

Casino sign on Fremont Street

The South Strip

For seven decades huge casinos have pushed ever further south along Las Vegas Boulevard, and what constitutes the South Strip has been repeatedly redefined. One thing has remained constant, however: entrepreneurs love to build lavish, eye-catching properties here because they're the first to be seen by drivers arriving from southern California. The current generation thus includes a scale model of Manhattan, New York–New York; the vast MGM Grand; fantasy castle Excalibur; an Egyptian pyramid, Luxor; and what's currently the true start of the Strip, gleaming tropical paradise Mandalay Bay. Thanks to successive buyouts and mergers, all these five are now owned by MGM Resorts and run as a cohesive unit. The exception, ageing Tropicana, has, not surprisingly, struggled to keep up.

Mandalay Bay

MAP P.26, POCKET MAP B7
3950 Las Vegas Blvd S ☎ 877 632 7700,
ⓦ mandalaybay.com.

The southernmost mega-casino on the Strip, **Mandalay Bay**, consists of two golden skyscrapers that tower over a sprawling complex covering a greater area than any other single property in Las Vegas. Linked to Luxor (see page 25) and Excalibur (see page 28) by a stand-alone outdoor **monorail** as well as indoor walkways, it belongs to the same owners, MGM Resorts. It was built in 1999 to provide a more sophisticated alternative to what were then its more overtly child-oriented neighbours, and apart from the **Shark Reef** aquarium (see page 25) offers little to lure in casual sightseers.

Beyond a certain vague tropical theming, there's no significance to the name "Mandalay". Instead Mandalay Bay's strongest selling point is its nightlife, with a high-end array of restaurants, bars, clubs – such as *Light* (see page 36), the first nightclub to be run under the auspices of Cirque du Soleil –

and music venues, including the prestigious *House of Blues* (see page 36), plus the self-explanatory Cirque show, *Michael Jackson One*. To keep its young, affluent guests on site during the day as well, there's also an impressively landscaped network of pools and artificial beaches that includes a wave pool and the "toptional" **Moorea Beach Club**.

Being further south of the Strip's centre of gravity than anyone would choose to walk, Mandalay Bay can feel a little stranded. Forced to work hard to attract and keep visitors, however, it managed to prosper through the recession. Inevitably, some of its restaurants have lost their original buzz, while the Mandalay Place mall has little to lure shoppers based elsewhere. For a night out, though, or a weekend in a self-contained luxury resort, Mandalay Bay can still match the best Las Vegas has to offer.

Incidentally, the *Four Seasons* hotel is right here too – its rooms occupy the top five floors of Mandalay Bay's original tower.

Shark Reef

MAP P.26, POCKET MAP B8
Mandalay Bay, 3950 Las Vegas Blvd ☎ 702 632 4555, ⓦ sharkreef.com. June–Aug daily 10am–10pm; Sept–May Mon–Thurs & Sun 10am–8pm, Fri & Sat 10am–10pm. Adults $25, ages 4–12 $19.

In keeping with Las Vegas's emphasis on immediate thrills, the **Shark Reef** aquarium focuses almost exclusively on dangerous marine predators, prowling through tanks designed to resemble a decaying ancient temple that's sinking into the sea. The species on show – largely chosen for their scary teeth and deadly stings – include giant crocodiles and Komodo dragons, as well, of course, as enormous sharks. Separate eerily illuminated cylindrical tanks are filled with menacing-looking jellyfish.

Shark Reef is located right at the back of Mandalay Bay; to reach it, you have to walk along several hundred yards of internal corridors, beyond the two convention centres.

Luxor

MAP P.26, POCKET MAP B6
3900 Las Vegas Blvd S ☎ 702 262 4000, ⓦ luxor.com.

The huge **Luxor** pyramid, with its sloping, monolithic walls of black shiny glass, was built in 1993 as the follow-up to the much more fanciful Excalibur (see page 28) next door. Originally it was filled to bursting with ancient Egyptian motifs, including not only a replica of King Tut's tomb but even an indoor River Nile. Then, when Las Vegas (and owners MGM Resorts in particular) decided to gear itself less towards kids and more towards adults, much of Luxor's archeological theming was stripped away. Nothing can mask the fact that it's a colossal pyramid, though, and Luxor today seems to be in an odd sort of limbo, embarrassed about its Egyptian past but unable to find an alternative identity.

Visitors who venture this far down the Strip – especially those arriving on the **Mandalay**

The Luxor Pyramid

The South Strip

BUFFET
Bayside Buffet — 10

RESTAURANTS
America — 6
Aureole — 11
Bacio (on Upper level) — 7
Border Grill — 12
China Tang — 4
Emeril's New Orleans
  Fish House — 2
Fleur — 9
Hussong's Cantina — 8
Il Fornaio — 5
Michael Mina Pub 1842 — 3
Tom Colicchio's Craftsteak — 1

EAST HARMON AVENUE

CITY CENTER

Hawaiian Marketplace

CVS

MONTE CARLO/ PARK MGM

Walgreen's

Hard Rock Café

UA Cinemas

CSI: The Experience

PARK AVENUE

The Park

Coca-Cola Store

MGM GRAND

T-Mobile Arena

M&Ms World

The Mansion

Arcade & The Big Apple Coaster (Second floor)

Brooklyn Bridge

MGM GRAND STATION

NEW YORK– NEW YORK

WEST TROPICANA AVENUE

Statue of Liberty

EAST TROPICANA AVENUE

EXCALIBUR WAY

THE TROPICANA

STABLE ROAD

LUXOR DRIVE

Fun Dungeon — (Lower level)

EXCALIBUR

WEST RENO AVENUE

EAST RENO AVENUE

GILES ST

HAVEN ST

LUXOR

Titanic: the Artifact Exhibition (Atrium level)

Bodies...The Exhibition (Atrium level)

Sphinx

LUXOR DRIVE

Mandalay Place

W. HACIENDA AVE

E. HACIENDA AVE

EAST HACIENDA AVENUE

MANDALAY BAY

FOUR SEASONS

Moorea Beach Club

Shark Reef

LAS VEGAS BOULEVARD SOUTH

(THE STRIP)

MANDALAY BAY MONORAIL

EXCALIBUR

SHOPS
Las Vegas Premium
  Outlets (South) — 3
The Shoppes at
  Mandalay Place — 1
Town Square — 2

BARS & LOUNGES
Bar At Times Square — 1
Minus5 Ice Bar — 5
Nine Fine Irishmen — 2
Red Square Bar — 8

CLUBS & MUSIC VENUES
Centra — 4
Hakkasan — 3
House of Blues — 6
Light — 7

SHOWS
Blue Man Group — 4
  (on Atrium level)
Criss Angel –
  Mindfreak Live! — 5
Kà — 1
Tournament of Kings — 3
  (on Lower level)
Zumanity — 2

Little Church of the West

0 metres 250
0 yards 250

WEST RUSSELL ROAD

"Welcome to Fabulous Las Vegas" sign (0.5 mile), 2 (1.5 miles) ▽ & 3 (2.5 miles)

Bay–Excalibur monorail – still congregate outside to take photos of the enormous Sphinx that straddles the main driveway. Immediately inside the main doors, there's also a re-creation of the facade of the Egyptian temple of Abu Simbel. Beyond that, however, there's little to distinguish the main casino floor. In the absence of noteworthy restaurants or shops, Luxor is best known for its clubs and bars, including *Flight*, a great place to drink cocktails and party.

Immediately upstairs, the so-called Atrium Level is home to two permanent exhibitions – **Bodies** (see opposite) and **Titanic** – as well as a small food court. It's also the best vantage point from which to admire the pyramid's cavernous interior; only guests can access the higher levels.

Titanic: The Artifact Exhibition

MAP P.26, POCKET MAP A5
Atrium Level, Luxor, 3900 Las Vegas Blvd S ☎ 702 262 4400, Ⓦ luxor.com/en/entertainment/titanic. Daily 10am–10pm. $32, ages 4–12 $24, over-64s $30; audio guides $6 extra.

Held in an enclosed building upstairs in Luxor, **Titanic: The Artifact Exhibition** is the world's only permanent exhibition of items salvaged from the *Titanic*. Displays that also include mock-ups of the fabled Grand Staircase tell the full story of the great ship, from construction to destruction. Each visitor is invited to pose for a souvenir photo on the Staircase, and as you enter you receive a "boarding pass" named for a specific passenger. Only as you leave do you find out whether he or she survived the catastrophe.

Prize artefacts include the actual wheel at which the helmsman tried and failed to steer clear of the iceberg on April 14, 1912, and the Big Piece, a gigantic slab of side-hull that broke off C Deck as

Bodies...The Exhibition

the ship sank, and which was raised from the ocean floor in 1998.

Bodies...The Exhibition

MAP P.26, POCKET MAP A5
Atrium Level, Luxor, 3900 Las Vegas Blvd S ☎ 702 262 4400, Ⓦ luxor.com/en/entertainment/bodies-the-exhibition.html. Daily 10am–10pm, last admission 9pm. $32, ages 4–12 $24, over-64s $30; audio guides $6 extra.

You might expect **Bodies... The Exhibition** to be a gory horror show. In fact, despite the advertising images of goggle-eyed corpses, it provides a surprisingly serious museum-quality experience. You have to keep reminding yourself that what look like brightly coloured mannequins really are dead bodies that have been "plastinated" for permanent display. Some are posed as though in life, playing sports in perpetuity, others have been dissected to show particular features of their anatomy. Certain sections, like that in which an entire circulatory system, down to the tiniest capillary, has been teased out and dyed in different colours, have an astonishing beauty. The sight of fatally diseased organs displayed alongside healthy counterparts is much more sobering. Even if you've wandered in for a quick laugh, you may leave determined to change your life around – not that Las Vegas is necessarily the best place to start.

Excalibur

MAP P.26, POCKET MAP B4
3850 Las Vegas Blvd S ☎ 702 597 7777,
🌐 excalibur.com.

Built in 1990, **Excalibur** remains the most visible reminder of the era when Las Vegas briefly reinvented itself as a vast children's playground. With its jam-packed, multi-coloured turrets and ring of clunky battlements it doesn't so much look like a castle, as like a child's drawing of a castle – and to be more specific still, a drawing of Walt Disney's version of Sleeping Beauty's castle. In fact, the architect responsible, Veldon Simpson, who later went on to design both Luxor and the MGM Grand, had travelled around Europe visiting hundreds of real-life castles. He ultimately settled on the same model used by Disney, Neuschwanstein in Bavaria, a

whimsical hybrid of French château and stern German fortress. Only a nit-picker would mention that the original Excalibur was a sword, not a castle.

These days, Excalibur is less child-oriented than it used to be. Its primary function for current owners MGM seems to be a kind of gateway to draw visitors towards the southern end of the Strip, complementing the free monorail to Luxor (see page 25) and Mandalay Bay (see page 24), prominent outside, with an easy indoor walkway to those properties further back. You access that by heading onto the upper level from the casino, lured ever onwards along the corridor by boutiques and fast-food places.

As Excalibur generally offers some of the Strip's least expensive hotel rooms, it caters largely to low-budget tour groups and families. That can result in a slightly jarring clash between its remaining child-friendly Arthurian theming, which includes the jousting-and-serving-wenches dinner-show *Tournament of Kings* (see page 37), and blue-collar adult entertainment

The Tropicana

"Welcome to Fabulous Las Vegas"

Familiar no doubt from every Las Vegas movie or TV show you've ever seen, the "Welcome to Fabulous Las Vegas" sign is an obligatory photo op for every visitor, just over half a mile south of Mandalay Bay. To minimize the risk of accidents, only cars heading south, away from the city, can access the narrow patch in between the north- and southbound carriageways of the Strip. Don't try walking this far, least of all in summer.

such as *Dick's Last Resort* bar and the *Thunder From Down Under* male stripper revue. Its lowest level, below the casino floor, is occupied by the **Fun Dungeon** (daily 10am–10pm), a jumble of fairground stalls, carnival amusements and arcade games.

Much of the upstairs, officially known as the Castle Walk Level, is taken up by a huge **food court**, which includes a massive *Krispy Kreme* doughnut bakery – where all the kitchen action is open to passers-by – and a *Tropical Smoothie Café* outlet. It's also home to the frankly poor *Excalibur Buffet* and assorted souvenir "shoppes".

The Tropicana

MAP P.26, POCKET MAP C4
3801 Las Vegas Blvd S ☏ 702 739 3626,
ⓦ troplv.com.

Built in 1957, and standing proudly aloof a mile south of the Strip, the **Tropicana** swiftly became a byword for luxury. It was also renowned from the start as being in the pocket of the Mob, and spent twenty years under investigation for the "skimming" of casino profits, money laundering and other Mafia-related skulduggery.

Although it's now poised at the country's busiest crossroads, the Tropicana has long struggled to compete with its mighty MGM-owned neighbours – Excalibur (see page 28), the MGM Grand (see page 30), and New York–New York (see opposite). Barely rescued from bankruptcy in 2008, it was given a $125-million makeover intended to restore its tropical-playground image and add something of the feel of Miami's South Beach. Among the casualties of that process was its fabled topless revue, the Folies Bergère, which sadly ended its residency shortly before its fiftieth anniversary.

While it's looking much crisper and brighter than before, the Tropicana still can't match the latest Strip giants. Hopes that it would blossom as a nightlife destination have failed to materialize, and there is little to draw in sightseers, shoppers or diners. Instead it remains slightly apart, with its strongest feature being an extensive pool complex that's open to guests only.

New York–New York

MAP P.26, POCKET MAP B3
3790 Las Vegas Blvd S ☏ 702 740 6969,
ⓦ newyorknewyork.com.

The first, and arguably the best, of Las Vegas's modern breed of replica "cities", **New York–New York** opened in 1997. Its exterior consists of a squeezed-up, half-sized rendition of the Manhattan skyline as it looked in the 1950s. The interior, which makes no attempt to correspond to the specific "buildings" outside, holds a smaller than average casino, plus a dining and nightlife district intended to evoke Greenwich Village.

Despite the broad Brooklyn Bridge that stretches along the Strip sidewalk, and the Empire State and Chrysler buildings etched against the Nevada sky, the most iconic feature of the facade is the **Statue of Liberty**, facing the intersection

The Big Apple Coaster

with Tropicana Avenue. Unlike the other elements here it's actually twice the height of the real-life statue. This spot never hosted a replica of the World Trade Center, but ad hoc memorials appeared here after September 11, 2001.

New York–New York has lost much of its original playful theming in recent years. Sightseers once stepped off the Strip to find themselves in Central Park at night, with owls peeping down from the trees. Things are more serious these days, enlivened here and there with stylish Art Deco motifs.

New York–New York isn't served by any monorail, but pedestrians pass through one corner en route between the pedestrian bridges to Excalibur and the MGM Grand. Perhaps to tempt them to stay, the areas nearest the Strip host an abundance of bars, pubs and food outlets. Much of the second floor is taken up by the Arcade, a rather ramshackle assortment of sideshows, games and kids' attractions.

The Big Apple Coaster

MAP P.26, POCKET MAP B3
New York–New York, 3790 Las Vegas Blvd S

☎ 702 740 6616, ⓦ newyorknewyork.com.
Daily 10.30am–midnight. $15 first ride, $26 for an all-day Scream Pass.
From the moment you catch a glimpse of New York–New York, you'll almost certainly also see – and hear – the tiny little yellow cabs that loop and race around its skyscraper towers. Previously known first as the Manhattan Express, then simply as The Roller Coaster, and now re-renamed **The Big Apple Coaster**, it operates from a replica subway station on the casino's upper floor. Speeding at 67mph, plunging over 200ft and rolling like a jet fighter, it's a serious thrill ride no theme-park fan should miss.

MGM Grand

MAP P.26, POCKET MAP C3
3799 Las Vegas Blvd S ☎ 877 880 0880, ⓦ mgmgrand.com.
The enormous **MGM Grand** casino has been through many changes since it opened in 1993. Back then, it attracted huge publicity as the largest hotel in the world and the first to incorporate its own theme park. It was also the location of the legendary 1997 boxing fight during

which Mike Tyson bit Evander Holyfield's ear.

These days, however, the MGM Grand keeps a lower profile, and it would be hard to say quite what identity it's aiming for any more. All traces of the theme park have long since vanished, while only the general preponderance of green now recalls the property's initial *Wizard of Oz* theme. With its original 5005 rooms boosted by the addition of the three all-suite *Signature* towers, it's surpassed in size only by the Venetian-Palazzo combination. Only in Las Vegas could such a behemoth seem to blend into the background.

One reason for this may be that with so many guests on site, the MGM Grand simply doesn't need to lure visitors in. It still boasts a fabulous array of dining and entertainment options, which includes the stunning Cirque de Soleil show *Kà*, and the three Michelin-starred *Joël Robuchon Restaurant*, where the $545 Degustation Menu is said to be the world's most expensive prix fixes.

Over the last few years, MGM Resorts have undertaken a massive overhaul of the Grand that has so far seen more old things disappear than new ones emerge. Casualties have included the live lions previously displayed in a glass enclosure just off the Strip, and the once-popular veteran nightclub *Studio 54*.

CSI: The Experience

MAP P.26, POCKET MAP E2
MGM Grand, 3799 Las Vegas Blvd S
☎ 702 891 5749, ⓦ csiexhibit.com. Daily 9am–9pm, last admission 8pm. Ages 12 and over $31.50, ages 4–11 $24.50.
Set well back from the MGM Grand's Strip entrance, **CSI: The Experience** is perhaps the most enjoyable family attraction in Las Vegas. Trading on the worldwide success of the CSI TV franchise, it enables participants to investigate, and almost certainly solve, fictional murder mysteries.

Each ticket entitles you to solve a couple of possible cases, taking roughly an hour to examine the murder scene, test out various hypotheses in the lab, and come up with a solution. Assistants are on hand to help, though you don't interact with any actors.

CSI: The Experience

Shops

Las Vegas Premium Outlets (South)

MAP P.26, POCKET MAP B13
7400 Las Vegas Blvd S ☎ 702 896
5599, ⓦ premiumoutlets.com. Mon–Sat
9am–9pm, Sun 9am–8pm.

The sort of mall you might
find beside the highway on
the outskirts of any town in
America, Las Vegas Premium
Outlets (South), 3 miles south
of Mandalay Bay, offers no-frills,
no-nonsense shopping at Banana
Republic, Gap, Nike and the like.
For visitors with the use of a car,
it's not a bad option for picking up
everyday items to take back home.
There's a basic fast-food court, grill
and Italian-style pizzeria.

The Shoppes at Mandalay Place

MAP P.26, POCKET MAP B6
Mandalay Bay, 3930 Las Vegas Blvd S
☎ 702 632 7777, ⓦ mandalaybay.com.
Daily 10am–11pm; hours for individual
stores may vary.

Arranged along the indoor hallway
that connects Mandalay Bay with
Luxor – a fair walk from the centre
of either, and from the monorail
too – The Shoppes at Mandalay
Place does not rank among Las
Vegas's premier shopping malls.
Instead, it's a rather haphazard mix
of big names such as The Guinness
Store, Nike Golf and Swarovski,
and smart boutiques, galleries and
novelty stores, plus several bars
and restaurants.

Town Square

MAP P.26, POCKET MAP B13
6605 Las Vegas Blvd S ☎ 702 269 5001,
ⓦ mytownsquarelasvegas.com. Mon–Thurs
10am–9pm, Fri & Sat 10am–10pm, Sun
11am–8pm.

Especially popular with locals who
prefer to steer clear of the Strip,
Town Square, 3 miles south of
Mandalay Bay, is a rarity in Las
Vegas, designed to be experienced
as an outdoor "neighbourhood"
rather than an air-conditioned
enclave. Visitors from further afield
may be less enthused by its attempt
to evoke the feel of a "European
village". Big stores include Staples,
a Whole Foods supermarket and an
Apple Store that offers free wi-fi;
there are also some unremarkable
restaurants and a cinema.

Buffet

Bayside Buffet

MAP P.26, POCKET MAP B7
Mandalay Bay, 3950 Las Vegas Blvd S
☎ 702 632 7402, ⓦ mandalaybay.com.
Mon–Sun 7–11am $19, 11am–2.30pm $22,
4.45–9.45pm $33.

Mandalay Bay's buffet has a much
nicer setting than most of its Las
Vegas rivals, overlooking the resort's
pool, and open, when weather
permits, to breezes. Apart from
the wide range of desserts, though,
and the pre-cut deli sandwiches
at lunchtime, the food is not all
that amazing.

Restaurants

America

MAP P.26, POCKET MAP B3
New York–New York, 3790 Las Vegas Blvd S
☎ 702 740 6451, ⓦ newyorknewyork.com.
Daily 24hr.

While serious foodies will find
nothing remarkable about this
24-hour diner, it's a great place to
bring kids, or Las Vegas first-timers,
thanks to the colossal, cartoon-like
relief map of the USA that hangs
from the ceiling. Serving signature
dishes from all over the country,
from Alaskan salmon salad ($16) to
Kansas City ribs ($25), there's food
to match every appetite.

Aureole

MAP P.26, POCKET MAP B7
Mandalay Bay, 3950 Las Vegas Blvd S
☎ 702 632 7401, ⓦ aureolelv.com. Mon–
Sat 5.30–10.30pm.

Aureole

With its astonishing "wine tower", a 42ft vertical wine cellar that's accessed by flying, white-clad "wine angels", Chef Charlie Palmer's showcase restaurant is a real must-see. His contemporary American cooking is something special, with the menu divided into "Root", "Ranch" and "Surf". The filet mignon entrée costs $59, while baked salmon is $31.

Bacio

MAP P.26, POCKET MAP C4
Tropicana, 3801 Las Vegas Blvd S ☎ 702 739 2341, ⓦ troplv.com. Daily 7–12pm.
A relaxed place to go for breakfast. Bacio is on the pricey side but the food is very good (smoked salmon Benedict, or beef belly crepes, both $20). There are also lighter dishes such as Greek yoghurt and granola for $14.

Border Grill

MAP P.26, POCKET MAP B8
Mandalay Bay, 3950 Las Vegas Blvd S ☎ 702 632 7403, ⓦ bordergrill.com. Mon–Fri from 11am, Sat & Sun from 10am.
Serving light and zestful "modern Mexican" cuisine that's a perfect match for its sun-kissed indoor-outdoor setting, this poolside veteran serves lunchtime salads, tacos and *tortas* (flatbreads) for well under $20, and larger dinner plates like Yucatan pork or Asado chicken, both for $26. A three-course set dinner costs about $45 and the hugely popular weekend brunch $39.

China Tang

MAP P.26, POCKET MAP D3
MGM Grand, 3799 Las Vegas Blvd S ☎ 702 891 3110, ⓦ mgmgrand.com. Mon–Thurs & Sun 5pm–10pm, Fri & Sat 11.30am–10.30pm.
This colourful restaurant evokes the Tang dynasty, with a splash of old Shanghai glamour. The Cantonese cuisine is influenced by provincial dishes from Sichuan, Shanghai and Beijing. Try their dim sum (from $12), braised pork ribs ($28) or channel your inner Chinese emperor with the traditional roasted duck ($138, advanced order required).

Emeril's New Orleans Fish House

MAP P.26, POCKET MAP E2
MGM Grand, 3799 Las Vegas Blvd S

☎ 702 891 7374, ⊛ emerils.com. Daily 11.30am–10pm.
Rich New Orleans flavours in a modern setting, courtesy of TV chef Emeril Lagasse. As the name suggests, the emphasis is on seafood, with barbecue shrimp among appetizers ($18) and pecan-crusted redfish on the mains menu ($39), but you can also get seared chicken or a rib-eye steak. If you don't have a dinner reservation, they should be able to seat you after 9pm.

Fleur

MAP P.26, POCKET MAP B7
Mandalay Bay, 3950 Las Vegas Blvd S ☎ 702 632 7200, ⊛ mandalaybay. com. Mon–Fri 11am–10pm, Sat & Sun 11am–10.30pm.
There's much more to Hubert Keller's modern tapas restaurant than its notorious $5000 foie gras burger. Its sumptuous menu features exquisite dishes from all over the world, including Spanish-style grilled octopus ($22) and Greek herb-roasted leg of lamb ($48). Even the so-called "Large Plates" are pretty small, though, so it's no place to be counting your

Minus5 Ice Bar

pennies. Parties of four can "Tour the World" for $310.

Hussong's Cantina

MAP P.26, POCKET MAP B6
Mandalay Bay, 3930 Las Vegas Blvd S
☎ 702 632 6450, ⊛ hussongslasvegas.com.
Mon–Thurs & Sun 11am–10pm, Fri & Sat 11am–11pm.
An outpost of the Mexican original that's said to have invented the margarita, *Hussong's* is as much a bar as a restaurant. Yet the food itself is surprisingly good, with $15–20 flautas, fajitas and chimichangas, and $15 nachos. Don't miss the $6 grilled corn, which is dusted with cheese flakes.

Il Fornaio

MAP P.26, POCKET MAP B3
New York–New York, 3790 Las Vegas Blvd S ☎ 702 650 6500, ⊛ ilfornaio.com/ lasvegas. Restaurant Mon–Thurs & Sun 7.30am–11pm, Fri & Sat 7.30am–midnight; Panetteria daily 6am–5.30pm.
While *Il Fornaio* is open for decent Italian food pretty much round the clock, in-the-know locals love it best of all in the morning, when you can enjoy a wonderful sit-down breakfast or simply pop in to the separate deli/bakery next door for fresh bread and espresso coffee.

Michael Mina Pub 1842

MAP P.26, POCKET MAP D3
MGM Grand, 3799 Las Vegas Blvd S ☎ 702 891 3922, ⊛ mgmgrand.com. Mon–Fri 11.30am–10pm, Sat–Sun 10am–10pm.
Top Las Vegas chef Michael Mina keeps things simple with his take on the gastro pub, serving substantial $18–22 burgers and old-fashioned favourites like fish and chips ($26) or succulent St Louis ribs ($22/34), along with $8–11 Happy Hour "small plates" such as brisket sliders or lobster grilled cheese and a couple of dozen draught beers.

Tom Colicchio's Craftsteak

MAP P.26, POCKET MAP E2
MGM Grand, 3799 Las Vegas Blvd S ☎ 702

THE SOUTH STRIP

891 7318, Ⓦ craftsteaklasvegas.com. Mon–
Thurs & Sun 5–10pm, Fri & Sat 5–10.30pm.
Serious carnivores swear this
dinner-only steakhouse serves the
best beef in Las Vegas, in melt-in-
your-mouth inch-thick cuts. Order
a la cart; there's lobster salad ($39)
as an appetizer and steaks from
$40. Set menus range from $130
for domestic Angus beef to $350
for Japanese Wagyu surf & turf.

Bars and lounges

Bar at Times Square

MAP P.26, POCKET MAP B3
New York–New York, 3790 Las Vegas Blvd
S Ⓣ 702 740 6466, Ⓦ newyorknewyork.
com. Mon–Thurs 1pm–2am, Fri–Sun
11am–2.30am, showtime 8pm–2am. Cover
$10 standing, reserved seating Mon–Thurs
& Sun $15, Fri & Sat $25.
If you like your nights out
sophisticated or edgy, steer clear
of this raucous sing-a-long bar
alongside New York–New York's
main casino floor; if you prefer to
scream along at the top of your
voice as two pianists go head-to-
head, playing whatever requests
spring to their tipsy audience's
mind, you're in the right place.

Minus5 Ice Bar

MAP P.26, POCKET MAP B6
Mandalay Bay, 3930 Las Vegas Blvd S
Ⓣ 702 632 7714, Ⓦ minus5experience.
com. Mon–Thurs & Sun 11am–1am, Fri &
Sat 11am–2am. Cover varies, typically $25
including one drink.
This funny, gimmicky bar is exactly
what it says it is – everything is
made of ice, from walls to glasses
(though the couches are spread
with deer skins). Customers
are loaned jackets, gloves and
boots to tolerate the minus
5°C temperature.

Nine Fine Irishmen

MAP P.26, POCKET MAP C3
New York–New York, 3790 Las Vegas Blvd S
Ⓣ 702 740 3311, Ⓦ ninefineirishmen.com.
Daily 11am–11pm. Cover $5 Wed & Thurs,

$10 Fri & Sat.
A genuine Irish pub, shipped in
pieces from Ireland, celebrating
Irish beer, food and, in the evening,
music and dance too. A small
patio out on the Strip looks over
"Brooklyn Bridge". During the
weekday Happy Hour (Mon–Fri
2–5pm), Guinness and other beers
cost $5 per pint.

Red Square Bar

MAP P.26, POCKET MAP B7
Mandalay Bay, 3950 Las Vegas Blvd S
Ⓣ 702 632 7407, Ⓦ mandalaybay.com.
Mon–Thurs & Sun 4–11pm, Fri 4.30pm–
midnight, Sat 4pm–midnight.
Both a bar and a restaurant, *Red
Square* is designed to evoke all
things Russian – the decadence of
the tsars, the graphic style of the
Communist era and the icy chill
of the steppes. Unless you have a
real penchant for caviar, the food
is a bit too expensive to be worth
it, but the bar is great, with its
solid-ice counter-top and frozen
vodka vault.

Clubs and music venues

Centra

MAP P.26, POCKET MAP B6
Luxor, 3900 Las Vegas Blvd S Ⓣ 866 983
4279, Ⓦ luxor.com. Daily 24hr.
Located within the Luxor resort,
this round-the-clock bar is a great
place to enjoy some casual drinks
while you play poker or video
slot games. Must-see sporting
events are broadcast live from the
venue's screens.

Hakkasan

MAP P.26, POCKET MAP D3
MGM Grand, 3799 Las Vegas Blvd S
Ⓣ 702 891 7888, Ⓦ hakkasan.com.
Thurs–Sun 10.30pm–4am. Cover men
$30, women $20.
Said to be the largest club in the
world, an offshoot of what was
originally a Chinese restaurant in

Light

Mandalay Bay pulled off a real coup by hosting the first-ever Cirque du Soleil nightclub, designed to keep fans of its *Michael Jackson One* show dancing all night. Holding over two thousand clubbers, it features a mobile DJ booth that rises from the floor, plus live Cirque performers. In summer, *Daylight* (W daylightvegas.com), the beach club, stages outdoor pool parties and evening concerts.

London, this colossal, multi-level place incorporates two separate full-sized nightclubs, plus all sorts of dining rooms, ultra-lounges and private gardens; superstar DJs attract up to 7500 clubbers at weekends.

House of Blues

MAP P.26, POCKET MAP B6
Mandalay Bay, 3950 Las Vegas Blvd S
T 702 632 7600, W houseofblues.com.
Daily 7am–midnight.
The national *House of Blues* music chain has recently revamped its Las Vegas outlet, in the heart of Mandalay Bay. While retaining its funky, voodoo-esque feel, the capacity has been reduced to a more intimate 1300. Individual concerts are interspersed with longer artist residencies; thus Carlos Santana has been signed up for regular long-term stints, with ticket prices from $99.

Light

MAP P.26, POCKET MAP B7
Mandalay Bay, 3950 Las Vegas Blvd S
T 702 632 4700, W thelightvegas.com.
Wed, Fri & Sat 10.30pm–4am. Cover charge varies.

Shows

Blue Man Group

MAP P.26, POCKET MAP B6
Luxor, 3900 Las Vegas Blvd S T 702 262 4400, W blueman.com. Daily 7pm & 9.30pm. $65–130.
The hilariously postmodern Blue Men are Las Vegas favourites; kids love their craziness, adults their cleverness. Mute and lurid blue from head to toe, they combine paint-splashing, cereal-spewing clowning with pounding percussion and amazing visual effects.

Criss Angel – Mindfreak Live!

MAP P.26, POCKET MAP A6
Luxor, 3900 Las Vegas Blvd S T 702 262 4400, W luxor.com. Wed–Sun 7pm & 9.30pm. From $59.
Although *Mindfreak Live!* bears the Cirque brand, it's basically a showcase for everything Angel does best, blending close-up trickery with mind-blowing illusions to create a thrilling magic show. Beyond the pyrotechnics and heavy metal, he's essentially a hard-working, old-fashioned audience-pleaser.

Kà

MAP P.26, POCKET MAP D2
MGM Grand, 3799 Las Vegas Blvd S T 702 531 3826, W cirquedusoleil.com. Mon–Wed, Sat & Sun 7pm & 9.30pm. $65–250.
There's more martial-arts muscularity to this Cirque

spectacular than to their other, more ethereal offerings; sceptics are guaranteed to find the set-piece stunts enacted on its tilting, rotating stage absolutely jaw-dropping. Add in extraordinary puppetry and sumptuous costumes, and while the twins-in-jeopardy storyline may leave you unmoved, *Kà* is certain to expand your horizons.

Tournament of Kings

MAP P.26, POCKET MAP A4
Excalibur, 3850 Las Vegas Blvd S ☎ 702 597 7600, ⓦ excalibur.com. Mon & Fri 6pm, Wed, Thurs, Sat & Sun 6pm & 8.30pm. From $56.

This swashbuckling swords-and-slapstick supper show plunges family audiences into a jousting contest, complete with villainous black knights and maidens in peril. Ideal for anyone who'd rather eat chicken with their fingers than sit through Shakespeare.

Zumanity

MAP P.26, POCKET MAP B3
New York–New York, 3790 Las Vegas Blvd S ☎ 702 740 6815, ⓦ cirquedusoleil.com.

Mon & Sun 9.30pm, Tues, Fri & Sat 7pm & 9.30pm. $75–190. All shows over-18s only.
While the concept – Cirque goes sexy – may pique your curiosity, the reality is disappointing, undercutting the erotic potential of fit bodies performing astonishing feats with pratfalls and smut. At times, it looks amazing, but it's no substitute for Cirque at their peak.

Wedding chapel

Little Church of the West

MAP P.26, POCKET MAP C9
4617 Las Vegas Blvd S ☎ 702 739 7971, ⓦ littlechurchofthewest.com. Daily 8am–11pm.

This cute little chapel really is old, by Las Vegas standards; built for the Last Frontier casino in 1942, it has since migrated south to a spot half a mile beyond Mandalay Bay. With its tranquil garden, it feels a world away from the big-casino chapels. Packages range from the $209 "Let's Elope" to the $2975 "All-Inclusive VIP Package".

THE SOUTH STRIP

Little Church of the West

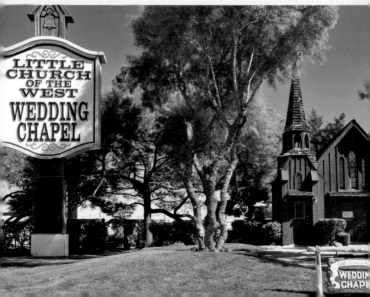

CityCenter and around

When MGM Resorts opened the CityCenter complex, in 2009, the aim was to add a whole new neighbourhood to Las Vegas, giving the city a new kind of sleek, corporate architecture. By building a self-contained enclave set back from the Strip, they would vastly increase the value of what was previously unused land, and finally make it possible to expand east–west. A massive financial gamble, the project involved a huge new casino, Aria; a high-end shopping mall, Crystals; and several hotel-and-condo skyscrapers. A new neighbourhood has indeed appeared, stretching from the open-air Park in the south, adjoining the Park MGM (with the NoMad Hotel occupying top floors), as far as the now-veteran Bellagio to the north. The one fly in the ointment is the brash new Cosmopolitan, cheekily added to the one tiny speck of Strip real estate that MGM didn't own.

Park MGM

MAP P.40, POCKET MAP C2
3770 Las Vegas Blvd S ☎ 702 730 7777,
ⓦ parkmgm.com.

With the unveiling of CityCenter, the low-profile **Monte Carlo** casino became increasingly prominent in the plans of owners MGM. The space between the former Monte Carlo and New York–New York has been transformed into a largely pedestrianized plaza known as **The Park**, and is home to the huge, multi-purpose **T-Mobile Arena**

The Park

(see page 47). In 2018, the Monte Carlo was re-branded as the **Park MGM**. Alongside the **Park Theater** concert venue (see page 47), the new complex houses an Italian marketplace, **Eataly**, with restaurants and food counters, and an almost 300-room boutique hotel, **NoMad**.

Crystals

MAP P.40, POCKET MAP B1 & F9
3720 Las Vegas Blvd S ☎ 702 590 9202, Ⓦ theshopsatcrystals.com.

As the one public component of CityCenter to abut the Strip, **Crystals** certainly catches the eye. Designed by Daniel Libeskind, its jagged, colourful facade makes a contrast with the white walls and air-conditioned cool of its interior. Its primary role is as a (hugely expensive) shopping mall, **The Shops at Crystals** (see page 44).

Purely as a spectacle, however, Crystals is well worth a quick walk-through. At one point, it was planned as an urban park, and it features some extravagant, playful wooden structures, including the intricate 70ft **Treehouse**, home to the stylish *Mastro's Ocean Club* restaurant (see page 45), as well as a pair of arching wooden "pods".

There's also plenty of water on show, including the swirling glass-encased **fountains** on the lower floor, and some dazzling **sculptures** of neon light.

The Cosmopolitan

MAP P.40, POCKET MAP F9
3708 Las Vegas Blvd S ☎ 702 698 7000, Ⓦ cosmopolitanlasvegas.com.

At first glance, most Las Vegas visitors assume that **The Cosmopolitan**, facing Planet Hollywood (see page 48) across the Strip, is just one more piece of the modernist jigsaw puzzle that comprises CityCenter. It's not; it's an entirely separate luxury casino-hotel, stacked up vertically rather than sprawling horizontally, and impishly squeezed atop the car park

Crystals

of the former Jockey Club (which MGM never managed to buy up), slap in front of CityCenter.

Since opening in 2010, the Cosmopolitan has made itself very much at home in this prime spot, seducing locals and tourists alike with its glitzy architectural flourishes, high-profile **Marquee** nightclub (see page 47), excellent array of appealing restaurants just steps away from the Strip, and general evocation of glamorous days gone by. In the evenings especially, its buzzing public spaces tend to jostle with excited crowds.

The Cosmopolitan is a throwback to the old Las Vegas, when each casino was separately owned and run, acted like the rest of the city didn't exist, saw its business as being all about gambling and nightlife rather than shopping, and aimed to keep visitors on site by making it all but impossible to find the exits. Be warned that the Cosmopolitan also has the last laugh on CityCenter: while you might understandably assume that you could simply walk all the way through the building and reach Aria (see page 41), you can't – there's no pedestrian through route.

CityCenter and around

FLAMINGO
LAS VEGAS

CAESARS PALACE

WEST FLAMINGO ROAD

| 0 | metres | 250 |
| 0 | yards | 250 |

FRANK SINATRA DRIVE

Grand
Bazaar
Shops

Bellagio Gallery
of Fine Art

BELLAGIO

The Fountains
of Bellagio

Eiffel
Tower PARIS

The Conservatory

Montgolfier
Balloon

Arc de
Triomphe

N

JOCKEY CLUB

PLANET
HOLLYWOOD

VDARA

THE
COSMOPOLITAN

CITYCENTER MONORAIL

WEST HARMON AVENUE

CITY
CENTER

Crystals

Treehouse

ARIA

VEER
TOWERS

CITYCENTER PLACE

Poker
Room

MANDARIN
ORIENTAL

Hawaiian
Marketplace

LAS VEGAS BOULEVARD SOUTH (THE STRIP)

BELLAGIO DRIVE

Aria
Convention Center

CVS

PARK MGM

Walgreen's

UA Cinemas

Hard Rock
Café

Coca-Cola
Store

T-Mobile Arena

PARK AVENUE

The Park

NEW YORK BLVD.

NEW YORK–
NEW YORK

M&Ms
World

MGM
GRAND

SHOP

| The Shops at Crystals | 1 |

BUFFETS

The Buffet at Aria	13
(on Promenade level)	
Buffet Bellagio	2
Wicked Spoon (on Level 2)	8

RESTAURANTS

Bellagio Patisserie	5
China Poblano (on Level 2)	7
Estiatorio Milos (on Level 3)	9
Javier's	12
Julian Serrano	10
Mastro's Ocean Club	11
Michael Mina	4
Noodles	3
Picasso	1
Scarpetta (on Level 3)	6

SHOW

| 0 | 1 |

BAR & LOUNGE

| Chandelier (on Levels 1 & 2) | 2 |

CLUBS & MUSIC VENUES

Marquee (on Levels 2 & 17)	3
Park Theater	4
Rose. Rabbit. Lie (on Level 2)	1
T-Mobile Arena	5

Aria

MAP P.40, POCKET MAP B1

3730 Las Vegas Blvd S ☎ 702 590 7111,
Ⓦ aria.com.

Although the CityCenter "neighbourhood" is supposed to be easy to explore on foot, you're only likely to visit **Aria**, the casino at its heart, if you make a very deliberate effort to reach it. Pedestrians can get here outdoors by following its hot, exposed approach road 250 yards west from the Strip, or more comfortably indoors, via the Crystals mall or the much longer walkways through Bellagio (see page 42) and the Park MGM (see page 38). A gleaming sci-fi **monorail** also connects Aria with both those properties, but the stations are so far back from the Strip that you gain very little by using it.

From the outside, with its sleek, curving skyscrapers, Aria looks more like a sophisticated big-city corporate HQ than a casino. The traffic circle in front of its main entrance features a pulsating **fountain**, while to the left, more water cascades down a sleek, glistening black wall, 24ft tall.

Aria also identifies itself more with, say, Chicago than Las Vegas, by eschewing billboards, video screens and neon in favour of prestigious **contemporary art**. Sculptors represented include Henry Moore, one of whose signature abstractions stands in the tiny gap between Aria and Crystals; Claes Oldenburg, responsible for the giant typewriter eraser near the Strip; Antony Gormley, whose *Feeling Material* hangs from the ceiling; and Maya Lin, whose 84ft silver casting of the Colorado River stretches above the check-in desks.

While Aria's dazzling modernism is certainly a welcome contrast with traditional Las Vegas aesthetics, in the end, of course, it's all in the service of Mammon – and more specifically, gambling. There's plenty more cutting-edge design to admire as you walk through the casino proper – don't miss the **Poker Room**, fringed by gigantic golden playing cards – but there's little reason to linger unless your intention is to gamble.

Both the upper and lower levels of Aria hold a fine roster of restaurants, bars and cafés, but

Aria casino

there are very few shops. Devoid of slots and gaming tables, the upper level can feel cavernously empty unless the **Convention Center** is in full swing.

When Aria opened it was home to a Cirque du Soleil tribute show to Elvis Presley. An unlikely fit for such a forward-looking property, the show swiftly ended its run, as did its replacement, Cirque's **Zarkana**. With the showroom now closed, Aria has shifted its focus to the Park Theater instead.

Bellagio

MAP P.40, POCKET MAP F7
3600 Las Vegas Blvd S ☎ **702 693 7111,**
ⓦ **bellagio.com.**

Ranking high among Las Vegas's absolute must-see casinos, **Bellagio** proudly surveys the Strip across the graceful dancing fountains of its own broad, semicircular lake. This cream-coloured vision of Italian elegance was unveiled in 1998 as the final great flourish of the twentieth century's fastest-growing new city. It was the handiwork of legendary entrepreneur Steve Wynn, who spared no expense in his bid to follow his success with the Mirage (see page 62) by building the greatest hotel the world had ever seen. His original idea was to model it on a French Mediterranean beach and call it Beau Rivage; that changed after he visited the village of Bellagio, beside Lake Como in Italy.

Although Wynn himself is no longer at the helm – when MGM bought out his Mirage corporation in 2000, he took the money and ran down the street to start again – Bellagio is still going strong, racking up the highest turnover and biggest profits in the city. It's also larger than ever, having thrust a tentacle southwards to create an indoor walkway down to CityCenter. As Bellagio's northeast corner is just a few steps across a pedestrian bridge from Caesars Palace (see page 51), many sightseers use it as a corridor to stay out of the sun as they head south, creating a constant flow of visitors.

Almost all of Bellagio's Strip facade is taken up with waterfront restaurants, so once you're inside you won't see much of the lake. Similarly, its colonnaded pool area

Musical fountains at Bellagio

is only open to guests. Even so, the sheer opulence of the main casino floor is astounding, and several of the public areas should not be missed. In addition to the **Conservatory**, be sure to walk through the hotel lobby, where a vast chandelier of multicoloured glass flowers, created by sculptor Dale Chihuly, swarms across the ceiling. And take a glance behind the check-in counter to see the Roman gardens, accessible to employees only.

When Bellagio first opened, the management briefly attempted to impose a dress code and bar the children of non-guests. Las Vegas's democratic open-to-all traditions soon put paid to that policy, however, so there's nothing snooty about the crowds you'll see window shopping in the exclusive stores of the small Via Bellagio shopping arcade, or gasping at the menu prices for its magnificent but undeniably expensive restaurants. Other than the building itself, the two most popular attractions that bring in visitors from elsewhere are the **buffet** (see page 44) and Cirque du Soleil's long-running, breathtaking water spectacular, **O** (see page 47).

The Fountains of Bellagio

MAP P.40, POCKET MAP F7
Bellagio, 3600 Las Vegas Blvd S. Mon–Fri 3–8pm every 30min, 8pm–midnight every 15min; Sat noon–8pm every 30min, 8pm–midnight every 15min; Sun 11am–3pm every 15min, 3–8pm every 30min, 8pm–midnight every 15min. Free.

Even when it's lying dormant, Bellagio's ice-blue eight-acre lake makes an impressive spectacle in the Nevada desert. When it erupts into a balletic extravaganza of jetting **fountains**, as it does from morning/early afternoon until midnight daily, it's the best free show in town. The sky-high spurts and streams are accompanied by booming music – mostly songs from Broadway

shows and popular classics. For anyone other than diners in the expensive waterfront restaurants the best views are from the Strip sidewalk (stake your place early), the top of the Eiffel Tower in Paris (see page 49) or from the guest rooms in either Paris (see page 48) or the Cosmopolitan (see page 39).

The Conservatory

MAP P.40, POCKET MAP E8
Bellagio, 3600 Las Vegas Blvd S. Open 24hr. Free.

Ever since Bellagio opened, its magnificent **Conservatory** has been considered one of the major sights of the city. A glassed-over courtyard ringed by galleries and restaurants, it's repeatedly transformed by a huge team of gardeners into extravagant, themed shows that include bizarre whimsical props amid an extraordinary array of living plants. The five separate seasonal displays start with the Chinese New Year and then celebrate spring, summer, autumn and winter. During the week it takes to dismantle each show and prepare the next, there's nothing to see.

Bellagio Gallery of Fine Art

MAP P.40, POCKET MAP E7
Bellagio, 3600 Las Vegas Blvd S ☎ 702 693 7871, ⓦ bellagio.com. Daily 10am–7pm. $14.

Originally home to Steve Wynn's own art collection, the **Bellagio Gallery of Fine Art** managed to survive Wynn's departure and continues to put on changing exhibitions that generally last for around six months. The entrance fee is high for such a small space though, and only worth paying for the better shows, such as a previous display of twenty paintings by Claude Monet, which was curated in conjunction with the Museum of Fine Arts in Boston.

Shop

The Shops at Crystals

MAP P.40, POCKET MAP F9
3720 Las Vegas Blvd S ☎ 702 590 9202,
ⓦ simon.com/mall/theshops-at-crystals.
Mon–Thurs 10am–11pm, Fri–Sun 10am–midnight.

Pitched at Las Vegas's proverbial "whales"– high-rolling big spenders – the glitzy Shops at Crystals makes no bones about being very high-end indeed. With its sparkling white walls, and exquisite sculptural features, few dare stray into boutiques belonging to designers such as Karl Lagerfeld.

Buffets

The Buffet at Aria

MAP P.40, POCKET MAP A2
Promenade Level, Aria, 3730 Las Vegas
Blvd S ☎ 702 590 7111, ⓦ aria.com.
Breakfast Mon–Fri 7–9am $25; brunch
Mon–Fri 9am–3pm $29; brunch Sat & Sun
7am–3pm $34; dinner daily 3–10pm, Mon–Thurs $39, Fri–Sun $44.

Choices at CityCenter's one buffet are more limited than elsewhere, but the food is a cut above. The sushi and Indian specialities are excellent and the desserts are the best in town. Pay $13 extra for unlimited beer, wine, champagne or Bloody Marys. An entire lobster is served at your table during weekend dinners.

Buffet Bellagio

MAP P.40, POCKET MAP E7
Bellagio, 3600 Las Vegas Blvd S ☎ 702 791
7111, ⓦ bellagio.com. Breakfast Mon–Fri
7–11am $25; lunch Mon–Fri 11am–3pm
$27; dinner Mon–Thurs 3–10pm $39; brunch
Sat & Sun 7am–3pm $34 (or $45 with
champagne); dinner Fri–Sun 3–10pm $44.

The first "gourmet buffet" in town sparked standards, and less happily prices, to rise all over Las Vegas. While no longer quite as exceptional, it still features an amazing array of food. For breakfast you can have salmon smoked or baked, and omelettes cooked to order, with fillings such as crabmeat.

Wicked Spoon

MAP P.40, POCKET MAP J6
Level 2, The Cosmopolitan, 3708
Las Vegas Blvd S ☎ 877 893 2001,
ⓦ cosmopolitanlasvegas.com. Brunch
Mon–Thurs 8am–5pm $28, Fri–Sun
8am–3pm $36; dinner Mon–Thurs 5–9pm
$42; Fri & Sun 3–9pm $49.

Although the Cosmopolitan's buffet is hard to find, right at the back upstairs, plenty of visitors make their way here to enjoy a wide range of carefully prepared cuisines. Most are served as individual portions, though you can take as many as you like. There's no breakfast; fill up with a late-morning brunch instead.

Restaurants

Bellagio Patisserie

MAP P.40, POCKET MAP E8
Bellagio, 3600 Las Vegas Blvd S, ☎ 702
693 8865, ⓦ bellagio.com. Mon–Thurs
6am–11pm, Fri–Sun 6am–midnight. No
reservations.

It takes real self-discipline to walk past the delectable Bellagio Patisserie. Start your day with a breakfast of pastries, omelettes and freshly brewed coffee. For lunch tuck into sandwiches, with crepes for dessert, and sweeten your journey home with a box of macarons or tasty chocolates.

China Poblano

MAP P.40, POCKET MAP K6
Level 2, The Cosmopolitan, 3708 Las Vegas
Blvd S ☎ 702 698 7900, ⓦ chinapoblano.
com. Mon–Thurs & Sun 11.30am–11pm, Fri
& Sat 11.30am–11.30pm.

The concept of combining Asia and Mexico goes back a long way – *china poblana* is the national dress of Mexico. Here, in what looks like a street café, it is Chinese and Mexican cuisines that are blended.

Bellagio Patisserie

Try the $19.88 Twenty Vegetable
Fried Rice dish (fried rice, egg,
pea shoots and twenty seasonal
vegetables); see if you can count
them all.

Estiatorio Milos

MAP P.40, POCKET MAP K7
Level 3, The Cosmopolitan, 3708 Las Vegas
Blvd S ☏ 702 698 7930, ⓦ milos.ca. Sun–
Thurs 12–3.30pm and 4–11pm, Fri–Sat
4pm–midnight.
Vast urns and exquisite statues
adorn this beautiful Greek
restaurant. For lunch there's a
fantastic $29 set menu; in the
evening your choice from the array
of fresh fish, flown in daily from
Athens, will arrive at your table
cooked to perfection, from $55
per person.

Javier's

MAP P.40, POCKET MAP B1
Casino Level, Aria, 3730 Las Vegas Blvd
S ☏ 866 590 3637, ⓦ aria.com. Daily
11.30am–midnight.
Spectacular Mexican restaurant,
complete with terrifying wooden
carvings, that serves all the standard
dishes, scrupulously prepared, for
around $20. A build-your-own-

tacos plate for two costs over $50,
inventive variations such as lobster
enchiladas cost just over $30, and
shrimp, steak and seafood mains
are around $50.

Julian Serrano

MAP P.40, POCKET MAP F9
Casino Level, Aria, 3730 Las Vegas Blvd S
☏ 877 230 2742, ⓦ aria.com, Mon–Thurs
& Sun 11.30am–10.30pm, Fri & Sat
11.30am–11pm.
One of Las Vegas's biggest hits of
recent years, this beautiful tapas
bar tastes even better than it looks.
Most tapas cost about $20 for a
small portion; be sure to branch
out and sample fabulous creations
like the cocoa butter balls filled
with chilled gazpacho. Larger
mains include paella for two from
about $50.

Mastro's Ocean Club

MAP P.40, POCKET MAP B1
Crystals, 3720 Las Vegas Blvd S ☏ 702 798
7115, ⓦ mastrosrestaurants.com. Daily
5–11pm.
Even the new Las Vegas still has a
penchant for a good old-fashioned
steakhouse, though this one stands
out not so much for its heavy-duty

CITYCENTER AND AROUND

$50-plus rib-eyes as its amazing setting. Reserve early and you get to dine in the bowers of Crystals' whimsical wooden Treehouse.

Michael Mina

MAP P.40, POCKET MAP E8
Bellagio 3600 Las Vegas Blvd S ☎ 702 693 7223, ⓦ michaelmina.net. Mon–Sat 5–9.45pm.

In his flagship restaurant adjoining Bellagio's Conservatory, Egyptian-born Michael Mina continues to reinvent his tried and tested classics. Starters such as tuna tartare with mint cost up to $28, while mains range from $56 (filo-crusted sole is $58) to Mina's signature lobster pot pie at $88. The chef's tasting menu costs $128 and the vegetarian version $85, with wine pairing an extra $70 per person.

Noodles

MAP P.40, POCKET MAP F8
Bellagio, 3600 Las Vegas Blvd S ☎ 702 693 8865, ⓦ bellagio.com. Daily 11am–2am.

Bellagio's casual, walk-ins only, pan-Asian diner, off the main casino floor behind the *Baccarat* bar, is well worth seeking out. Its intriguing decor sets a cosy tone and the food, ranging from Thai to Vietnamese, to Chinese and Japanese, is no disappointment. Noodle dishes are around $20 and at weekend lunchtimes dim sum typically costs around $10.

Picasso

MAP P.40, POCKET MAP F7
Bellagio, 3600 Las Vegas Blvd S ☎ 702 693 8865, ⓦ bellagio.com. Mon, Wed & Sun 5.30–9.30pm.

This elegant two-Michelin star restaurant has a beautiful view of the Bellagio fountains and original Picassos on its walls. Chef Julian Serrano offers a small selection of amazing French dishes that change seasonally, while the wine cellar is stocked with bottles from the finest European vineyards. You may spend around $400 for an unforgettable meal for two.

Scarpetta

MAP P.40, POCKET MAP K7
Level 3, The Cosmopolitan, 3708 Las Vegas Blvd S ☎ 702 698 7960, ⓦ cosmopolitanlasvegas.com. Daily 6–11pm.

Courtesy of "New Italian" chef Scott Conant, the food is even better than the view at *Scarpetta*, which has huge windows overlooking the Bellagio fountains. All of Las Vegas has flocked to enjoy starters like his $19 tuna "susci", and mains including short rib and bone marrow agnolotti (stuffed pasta, $26). For the full works, go for the $125 tasting menu.

Scarpetta

Bar and lounge

Chandelier

MAP P.40, POCKET MAP K6 & F9
Cosmopolitan, 3708 Las Vegas Blvd S
☎ 702 698 7979, ⓦ cosmopolitanlasvegas.
com. Casino level open 24hr, other levels
hours vary.

Beneath the dazzling, dangling
canopy of the eponymous two-
million-crystal chandelier, the
Cosmopolitan's centrepiece bar
soars through three separate levels.
It's the middle floor where the
action is, with DJ music and a
buzzy crowd.

Clubs and music venues

Marquee

MAP P.40, POCKET MAP F9 & K6
Levels 2 and 17, The Cosmopolitan,
3708 Las Vegas Blvd S ☎ 702 333 9000,
ⓦ marqueelasvegas.com. Nightclub Mon
& Fri-Sat 10pm-4am; Dayclub daily
10am-7pm in summer. Cover varies
$35-100.

This cutting-edge indoor-outdoor
nightclub with a pool-centred
"dayclub", features a 50ft-high
main floor, the Boombox,
overlooking the Strip, and the
Library, which has pool tables. The
dayclub is smaller than at Encore
(see page 67), but attracts
bigger-name DJs and celebrities.
Add in drinks and the dollars
add up; buy a wristband for the
whole weekend.

Park Theater

MAP P.40, POCKET MAP B2
Park MGM, 3770 Las Vegas Blvd S ☎ 844
600 7275, ⓦ parkmgm.com. See website
for schedule.

Five-thousand-seat indoor arena,
with a larger stage than the
Colosseum at Caesars Palace, that's
primarily used for live music. So
far it's hosted residencies by the
likes of Cher, Stevie Wonder and
Sting, with prices ranging from
$110-460.

Rose. Rabbit. Lie

MAP P.40, POCKET MAP J6
Level 2, The Cosmopolitan, 3708
Las Vegas Blvd S ☎ 702 698 7440,
ⓦ cosmopolitanlasvegas.com. Wed-Sat
6pm-midnight; charge for special events.

Self-proclaimed "modern
supper club", targeted at The
Cosmopolitan's hipster clientele,
that remains deliberately hard to
categorize. Having abandoned the
avant-garde performance-art show
with which it opened, it now stages
retro-style gigs and one-off events,
and serves excellent cocktails and
bar food.

T-Mobile Arena

MAP P.40, POCKET MAP A3
3780 Las Vegas Blvd S ☎ 702 692 1600,
ⓦ t-mobilearena.com. See website for
schedule.

Set back from the Strip between
New York–New York and the
Park MGM, this huge covered
stadium was unveiled in 2016
as the centrepiece of The Park
development. Holding twenty
thousand spectators, and home to
the Vegas Golden Knights hockey
team, it has put on gigs by Kanye
West, Justin Timberlake and
Metallica, plus boxing matches,
basketball games and award
ceremonies. Concert tickets range
from $60-280.

Show

O

MAP P.40, POCKET MAP E7
Bellagio, 3600 Las Vegas Blvd S ☎ 702 693
8866, ⓦ cirquedusoleil.com. Wed-Sun 7pm
& 9.30pm. $99-217.

This phenomenal show centres
on a metal-mesh stage, any part
of which can suddenly disappear
beneath the performers' feet. The
dazzling array of death-defying
leaps and plunges create a visual
spectacular you'll never forget.

The Central Strip

Long the scene of fierce inter-casino rivalries, the central portion of the Strip now feels much more like a pedestrian neighbourhood, where visitors stroll from one casino to the next thanks to new outdoor spaces like the Linq development, adjoining the Flamingo and the Roman Plaza outside Caesars Palace. What's not obvious, however, is that all those casinos, from the block-spanning Caesars Palace to grizzled veterans like the Flamingo and Harrah's across the Strip, and newcomers like Paris and Planet Hollywood to the south, now belong to the same conglomerate – and you'd never guess it was Harrah's that came out on top.

Planet Hollywood

MAP P.50, POCKET MAP G9
3667 Las Vegas Blvd S ☏ 866 919 7472,
Ⓦ caesars.com/planet-hollywood.

The only Strip giant saddled with a brand name not otherwise known for gambling, **Planet Hollywood** has struggled to establish a strong identity; it's not part of the dining chain or even an independent entity. The building itself opened in 2000 as a new version of the long-established Aladdin, where Elvis Presley married Priscilla in 1966. Planet Hollywood took it over in 2004, after the Aladdin went broke in the wake of 9/11, but they in turn soon floundered and sold out to Harrah's in 2010.

Planet Hollywood subsequently raised its profile by signing Britney Spears for a long-term residency, which ended in 2017. As the Aladdin, though, it always seemed to be empty, thanks to the design flaw that meant the door from the Strip was too hard to find – simply rectified by erecting a huge sign reading "Casino Entrance". The main attraction within is the **Miracle Mile** mall (see opposite); the actual casino is relatively small, and is largely targeted, with its blaring music and flashing lights, at hip young visitors.

Miracle Mile

MAP P.50, POCKET MAP G8
Planet Hollywood, 3663 Las Vegas Blvd S
☏ 702 866 0704, Ⓦ miraclemileshopslv.
com.

Coiled like an enormous snake around and through Planet Hollywood, the **Miracle Mile** mall is nonetheless an entirely separate operation. Built at the same time as the new Aladdin, in 2000, and still bearing traces of its original Arabian Nights theming, it was credited by some as being responsible for the Aladdin's financial failure; given the chance to stroll into a mall without having to walk through a casino en route, Strip sightseers simply ignored the Aladdin altogether. Besides a free **"thunderstorm" attraction**, the Miracle Mile holds a wide range of bars, restaurants and theatres to complement the clothing boutiques, shoe shops and galleries (see page 56).

Paris

MAP P.50, POCKET MAP G8
3655 Las Vegas Blvd S ☏ 877 796 2096,
Ⓦ caesars.com/paris-las-vegas.

Designed by the architects previously responsible for New York–New York, and opened a few months before the millennium, **Paris** represented the final flourish of the Las Vegas craze for building entire miniature cities. Its exterior remains one of the Strip's most enjoyable spectacles, surmounted by a gigantic Eiffel Tower whose legs crash through the ceiling into the heart of the casino itself, and anchored by the Arc de Triomphe, the Opera and a Montgolfier hot-air balloon, which becomes a glowing landmark at night.

Although it's slightly misleading to think of Paris as a separate casino at all – it was originally built as an extension to Bally's (see page 51) next door, to which it's linked by a broad corridor at the back of the building – it was an immediate hit. With both of these properties now owned by Caesars Entertainment, the tail these days is clearly wagging the dog, and Bally's feels like a minor adjunct to Paris.

Pleasing Parisian touches, such as the ironwork that echoes the city's Metro stations, still abound throughout the interior. From the excellent **buffet** to the pastry shops and bridal-wear boutiques, the great majority of Paris's shops, restaurants and bars have some

sort of French connection. Much of it is tongue-in-cheek, so even the more tenuous links, as in calling the sports bar the **Bar du Sports**, are just part of the fun. The one area where visitors have balked at the Gallic flavour has been entertainment; Paris has long since abandoned its hopes of staging all-French productions (like, say, *Phantom of the Opera* or *Les Miserables*) in favour of safer options like the musical *Marilyn* or *I Love the '90s* show.

Eiffel Tower Experience

MAP P.50, POCKET MAP G8
Paris, 3655 Las Vegas Blvd S ☎ 888 727 4758, ⓦ caesars.com/paris-las-vegas. Daytime 10am–7pm, nighttime 7pm–1am. $16–$22.

Towering 540ft over the Strip, Las Vegas's version of the **Eiffel Tower** is half the height of the Seine-side original. It's not simply a half-sized replica, however; if it was, you wouldn't be able to squeeze into the elevators, for example. In addition, this one is made of steel not iron, and doesn't have a public staircase to the top.

Paris

The Central Strip

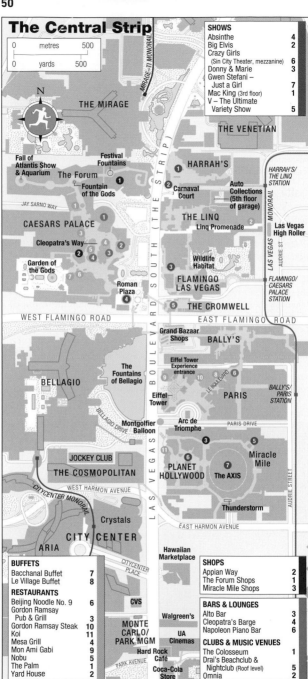

| metres | 0 | 500 |
| yards | 0 | 500 |

N

THE MIRAGE

THE VENETIAN

Fall of
Atlantis Show
& Aquarium
The Forum
Fountain
of the Gods

Festival
Fountains

HARRAH'S

Carnaval
Court

Auto
Collections
(5th floor
of garage)

HARRAH'S/
THE LINQ
STATION

JAY SARNO WAY

CAESARS PALACE

THE LINQ
Linq Promenade

Las Vegas
High Roller

Cleopatra's Way

Garden of
the Gods

Roman
Plaza

Wildlife
Habitat

FLAMINGO
LAS VEGAS

THE CROMWELL

FLAMINGO/
CAESARS
PALACE
STATION

WEST FLAMINGO ROAD

EAST FLAMINGO ROAD

Grand Bazaar
Shops

BALLY'S

Eiffel Tower
Experience
entrance

BELLAGIO

The
Fountains
of Bellagio

Eiffel
Tower

Montgolfier
Balloon

PARIS

BALLY'S/
PARIS
STATION

LE BOULEVARD

Arc de
Triomphe

PARIS DRIVE

JOCKEY CLUB

THE COSMOPOLITAN

WEST HARMON AVENUE

PLANET
HOLLYWOOD

Miracle
Mile

The AXIS

Thunderstorm

CITYCENTER MONORAIL

Crystals

CITY CENTER

ARIA

CITYCENTER
PLACE

EAST HARMON AVENUE

Hawaiian
Marketplace

CVS

Walgreen's

MONTE
CARLO/
PARK MGM

UA
Cinemas

Hard Rock
Café

PARK AVENUE

Coca-Cola
Store

SHOWS

Absinthe	4
Big Elvis	2
Crazy Girls	6
(Sin City Theater, mezzanine)	
Donny & Marie	3
Gwen Stefani –	
Just a Girl	7
Mac King (3rd floor)	1
V – The Ultimate	
Variety Show	5

BUFFETS

Bacchanal Buffet	7
Le Village Buffet	8

RESTAURANTS

Beijing Noodle No. 9	6
Gordon Ramsay	
Pub & Grill	3
Gordon Ramsay Steak	10
Koi	11
Mesa Grill	4
Mon Ami Gabi	9
Nobu	5
The Palm	1
Yard House	2

SHOPS

Appian Way	2
The Forum Shops	1
Miracle Mile Shops	3

BARS & LOUNGES

Alto Bar	3
Cleopatra's Barge	4
Napoleon Piano Bar	6

CLUBS & MUSIC VENUES

The Colosseum	1
Drai's Beachclub &	
Nightclub (Roof level)	5
Omnia	2

Visitors can either dine in the luxury restaurant 100ft up, or buy a ticket inside Paris's main entrance for the **Eiffel Tower Experience** and ride all the way to the summit viewing platform. While it offers great views all day long, the prime time to come is in the evening; as its builders always cheekily intended, the Eiffel Tower makes a perfect vantage point for watching the Bellagio fountains.

Bally's

MAP P.50, POCKET MAP G7
3645 Las Vegas Blvd S ☎ 877 603 4390, ⓦ caesars.com/ballys-las-vegas.

These days, you could easily fail to notice **Bally's**, set well back from the Strip opposite Bellagio. When it opened in 1973, however, this was the MGM Grand, the biggest hotel in the world. Only after a terrible hotel fire killed 84 people here in 1980 was it bought and renamed by the gaming manufacturer Bally's, and a new MGM Grand constructed further south. Now owned by Caesars Entertainment, Bally's has become a humdrum casino.

Bally's was built in the era when casinos still needed huge Strip-front car parks. Legendary in Las Vegas lore as the landing site for Nicolas Cage and the parachuting Elvises in the 1992 movie *Honeymoon in Vegas*, and subsequently spanned by a network of neon-covered walkways, the former Bally's car park has now at last been built over to become the site of an open-air mall, the **Grand Bazaar Shops**. The small booths and kiosks are largely devoted to snacks and souvenirs, so it's hardly a must-see attraction, but it's one more step towards making the Strip truly pedestrian-friendly.

Caesars Palace

MAP P.50, POCKET MAP F6
3570 Las Vegas Blvd S ☎ 866 227 5938, ⓦ caesarspalace.com.

Rod Stewart at The Colosseum

Still a Las Vegas headliner in its own right, fifty years since it was built, **Caesars Palace** remains arguably the biggest name on the Strip. During the casino-building spree either side of the millennium, it slipped for a moment behind its newer rivals, to the point where Harrah's Entertainment were able to buy up control. Recognizing the prestige value of the name, however, they've not only reinvigorated Caesars and put it back on top, but changed their own name to Caesars Entertainment.

Caesars Palace was originally the creation of **Jay Sarno**, a hard-gambling associate of legendary Teamsters leader Jimmy Hoffa. Cobbled together for just $24 million, it was unveiled in 1966, complete with clerks dressed as Roman centurions and cocktail waitresses kitted out like Cleopatra. Sarno himself doubled his money and sold out in 1969; he moved on to build Circus Circus, and eventually died of a heart attack in a suite at Caesars in 1984.

As well as coming up with the Caesars Palace name, designed to appeal to American and European gamblers alike, Sarno also decreed that the one thing it will never have is an apostrophe – it does not belong to Caesar, it's filled by the thousands of Caesars who choose to visit it. His crucial legacy, however, was that he'd set Caesars up on an expanse of land – originally rented from Kirk Kerkorian, who remained a major Las Vegas player until his death in 2015 – that has so far proved big enough to hold every enlargement architects have been able to imagine.

Pausing to admire Caesars Palace from the Strip is one of the great joys of visiting Las Vegas. White marble Classical statues are everywhere you look, from Julius Caesar forever hailing a cab on the main driveway to the Winged Victory of Samothrace guarding a row of gently cascading pools. Most impressive of all are the ornate fountains that surround the entrance to the Forum mall.

The central bulk of Caesars Palace is still proudly set back around 150 yards from the Strip; all that space between the casino and the Strip originally held an enormous car park. Once Las Vegas visitors began to arrive by plane instead of by car, the gap became a deterrent to pedestrians. It was Caesars that pioneered the use of long moving walkways to haul them in – and naturally neglected to build corresponding outbound walkways to let them back out again. Bit by bit, the space has been built over. First, at the northern end, the vast **Forum** mall (see opposite) steadily extended until it reached

all the way to the Strip; then the mighty **Colosseum** appeared alongside, in 2003; and more recently the **Roman Plaza** has burgeoned at the south, and now holds bars, restaurants and even, currently, a circus marquee, which is home to the *Absinthe* show (see page 60).

Inside, Caesars Palace bewilders most first-time visitors. Unlike newer Las Vegas properties, designed to be user-friendly and let you find what you're looking for, Caesars was laid out in the hope that gamblers might never be able to escape.

Making your way between the casino itself and the Forum is easy enough; the two simply meet on the casino floor. However, exploring the rest of Caesars Palace is less straightforward. A network of narrow and circuitous corridors lead to the older **Appian Way** mall, which offers the chance of a close-up inspection, from directly below, of Michelangelo's naked *David*, and Cleopatra's Way, home to the Egyptian-themed *Cleopatra's Barge* nightclub (see page 59).

Much of the rest of the property, including the luxurious **Garden of the Gods** pool complex, based on the baths of Pompeii, is only open to registered guests.

The Forum

MAP P.50, POCKET MAP F5
3500 Las Vegas Blvd S ☎ 702 893 3807,
Ⓦ simon.com/mall.

By opening the **Forum** mall in 1992, Caesars Palace not only became the first Strip casino to turn

The Buffet of Buffets

Buffet fans should watch out for the **Buffet of Buffets pass**, sold at the buffets in every Caesars-owned casinos (excluding Planet Hollywood), which allows 24-hour unrestricted access to them all for a cost of $60, or $75 on Fridays and Saturdays. Use it to eat at, say, 8pm one night, 7pm the next, and you get two dinners into the bargain. Note, however, that each visit to the *Bacchanal Buffet* at Caesars Palace costs extra.

The Cromwell

both shopping and dining into major reasons to visit Las Vegas, it also created one of the city's most iconic attractions.

Though widely copied ever since, the Forum's domed false-sky ceiling still packs a mind-blowing punch. Designed to evoke the skyline of ancient Rome, it cycles hourly between the dazzling blue of "day" and the orange glow of "night".

Sadly, though, many of the kitschier elements of the Forum's earlier years, such as the animatronic "living statues" that adorned its centrepiece fountains, have been discarded in favour of ever more opulent and ornate decor. The most striking feature these days is the amazing convoluted spiral escalator at the Forum's main Strip entrance. Its separate moving pathways follow different trajectories, so you can never be sure they'll take you where you want to go.

The **Forum Shops** themselves still rank as Las Vegas's premier shopping spot (see page 56).

The Cromwell

MAP P.50, POCKET MAP G7
3595 Las Vegas Blvd S ☎ 702 777 3777,
ⓦ caesars.com/cromwell.

Squeezed into a sandwich-sized slot at one of Las Vegas's prime intersections, the Strip's smallest casino used to be a budget alternative, known originally as the Barbary Coast and since 2007 as Bill's Gamblin' Hall & Saloon. It reopened in 2014, however, as a self-styled "boutique hotel", **The Cromwell**.

For no obvious reason, the name is intended to evoke Parisian splendour rather than those titans of English history, Thomas and Oliver. Its 188 rooms are now luxurious and expensive, while the principal new features are **Giada**, an Italian restaurant run by TV chef Giada de Laurentiis, and **Drai's** (see page 60), a massive indoor-outdoor rooftop club; the entire structure had to be strengthened to support the colossal weight of its various pools and pavilions.

Flamingo

Flamingo Las Vegas

MAP P.50, POCKET MAP G6
3555 Las Vegas Blvd S ☏ 702 733 3111,
ⓦ caesars.com/flamingo-las-vegas.
Now that it's just another glossy
casino, shoulder to shoulder in
the Strip's endless procession
of identikit giants, it's all but
impossible to picture **the Flamingo**
in its original form. Whatever
anyone may tell you, when it
opened in 1946 it wasn't the
very first Strip resort of them
all. Standing alone in the desert,
however, a mile south of its nearest
neighbour, the Last Frontier, the
Flamingo was an enticing hundred-
room oasis that put Las Vegas
on the map as a glamorous, even
dangerous, getaway.

Not that the Flamingo was an
immediate hit. So disastrously
over-budget that it was forced
to close within a fortnight, its
initial failure cost owner Benjamin
"Bugsy" Siegel his life, when his
fellow mobsters gunned him down
the next year. By then, however, the
Flamingo was already going strong,

and a wave of imitators was starting
to appear.

With Bugsy a distant, sanitized
memory, the Flamingo these days
is much more Donny and Marie –
long-term residents in its showroom
– than Don Corleone. Its current
owners, Caesars Entertainment,
target it largely at older visitors
who remember Las Vegas as it used
to be back in the 1980s, when the
Flamingo was still the biggest hotel
in the world, and before everything
had to keep reinventing itself to suit
the latest trend.

From its superb neon sign and the
Strip-facing patio of *Jimmy Buffet's
Margaritaville* at the front, to the
real-life flamingoes and penguins
in the free **Wildlife Habitat** and
garden-set pool complex around
the back, there's a lot to like
about the Flamingo. As The Linq
development next door expanded,
The Linq Promenade was born – a
dining, shopping and entertainment
district complete with a 550ft
observation wheel, located between
The Linq Hotel and Flamingo.

The Linq

MAP P.50, POCKET MAP G5
3535 Las Vegas Blvd S ☏ 800 634 6441,
ⓦ caesars.com/linq.
Caesars Entertainment responded
to MGM Resorts' construction of
CityCenter by carving out its own
rival "neighbourhood". Centring
on the showpiece High Roller, it
took what was previously a narrow
roadway between the Flamingo and
Imperial Palace casinos, and turned
it into a broader pedestrian corridor
of shops, bars and restaurants.

The long-standing Imperial Palace
was not demolished, but totally "re-
skinned", with its previous Japanese
facade stripped away and its
interior decor transformed. Briefly
re-christened the Quad, it has now
appropriated the name of the entire
project – **The Linq**.

New features include a 32-
lane bowling alley with its own
restaurant, plus a tattoo studio,

a "sneaker boutique" opened by rapper Nas, and several bars.

High Roller

MAP P.50, POCKET MAP H6
3545 Las Vegas Blvd S ☎ 702 322 0537, ⓦ caesars.com/linq. Daily 10.30am–2am. $22 11.30am–7pm, $37 7pm–2am.

The world's largest observation wheel, the **High Roller** stands just off the Strip at the far end of the pedestrianized Linq entertainment district. At 550ft, it's over a hundred feet taller than the similar, 443ft London Eye, and rotates non-stop. Each of its 28 see-through cabins can carry up to forty passengers. The long-range panoramas are spectacular, though intervening buildings mean it doesn't offer ground-level views of the Strip.

Harrah's

MAP P.50, POCKET MAP G5
3475 Las Vegas Blvd S ☎ 800 214 9110, ⓦ caesars.com/harrahs-las-vegas.
Harrah's is the great unsung success story of the Strip. When all its rivals were going crazy for adding eye-catching, child-friendly gimmicks, constructing replica cities and enticing young hipsters to day-night pool parties, Harrah's just carried on giving parents the same old, same old formula of cheap eats, plentiful slots and middle-of-the-road entertainment. And it did it all so well that one by one Harrah's swallowed up all of its Central Strip rivals. Then, having bought the lot, the Harrah's organization simply changed its name to Caesars Entertainment; it's as if it never happened.

For anyone under a certain age, Harrah's itself remains as boring as ever. Walk past on the Strip, and your attention may be captured by the performers on the open-air **Carnaval Court** stage, but step inside and you're in a soporific time warp, where country superstar Toby Keith's *I Love This Bar & Grill!* is the biggest attraction. To be fair, Harrah's does put on some good-value daytime shows, including *Mac King* (see page 61) and *Big Elvis* (see page 60), but it's no place for thrill-seeking sightseers.

The High Roller

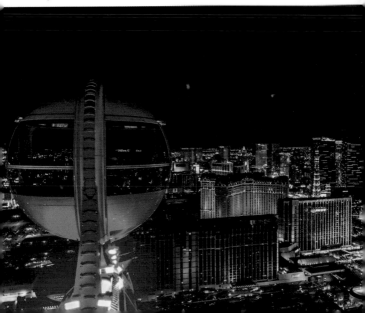

Shops

Appian Way

MAP P.50, POCKET MAP F6
Caesars Palace, 3570 Las Vegas Blvd S
📞 702 731 7222, 🌐 caesars.com/caesars-
palace. Store hours vary.

Much smaller than the Forum, the
Appian Way is arrayed along two
corridors just off the casino floor at
Caesars Palace. Centring on an 18ft
marble replica of Michelangelo's
David, it includes upscale jewellery
stores, high-end crafts at Martin
& MacArthur, and a shop selling
Caesars' merchandise.

The Forum Shops

MAP P.50, POCKET MAP F5
3500 Las Vegas Blvd S 📞 702 893 3807,
🌐 simon.com/mall. Mon–Thurs & Sun
10am–11pm, Fri & Sat 10am–midnight.

Still going strong after a quarter
of a century, The Forum Shops is
foot-for-foot the country's most
successful mall. That's partly
because its big-name brands tend
to be squeezed into smaller spaces
than usual. While its two main
"streets" are hardly full of surprises
– expect to see an Apple Store,

Gap and H&M, for example –
they do offer a very intense burst
of shopping.

Miracle Mile Shops

MAP P.50, POCKET MAP G8
Planet Hollywood, 3663 Las Vegas Blvd S
📞 888 800 8284, 🌐 miraclemileshopslv.
com. Mon–Thurs & Sun 10am–11pm, Fri &
Sat 10am–midnight.

Give or take the odd fountain,
the largest casino mall, the
Miracle Mile Shops, could be just
about anywhere. Easily entered
straight from the Strip, it really
is a mile long; walk from one
end to the other and you'll pass
a huge range of stores, from mall
staples like Urban Outfitters,
American Apparel, French
Connection and Quiksilver to
some jaw-droppingly awful "art
galleries" and a couple of ABC
convenience stores.

Buffets

Bacchanal Buffet

MAP P.50, POCKET MAP F6
Caesars Palace, 3570 Las Vegas Blvd S
📞 702 731 7928, 🌐 caesars.com/caesars-

Miracle Mile Shops

palace. Brunch Mon–Fri 7.30am–3pm $40, champagne brunch Sat & Sun 8am–3pm $55; dinner Mon–Fri 3–10pm $55, Sat & Sun 3–10pm $65.

Las Vegas's top-ranked gourmet buffet – the best at any Caesars-owned property – revolutionized the buffet concept. It features five hundred freshly made items daily, from sushi, dim sum and pho soup to oysters and wood-fired pizzas, prepared by chefs at nine separate "show kitchens".

Le Village Buffet

MAP P.50, POCKET MAP G7
Paris, 3655 Las Vegas Blvd S ☎ 702 946 7000, ⓦ caesars.com. Breakfast Mon–Fri 7–11am $22, Sat & Sun 7–10am $24; lunch Mon–Fri 11am–3pm $25; champagne brunch Sat & Sun 10am–3pm $31; dinner Mon–Thurs & Sun 3–10pm $31, Fri & Sat 3–10pm $31.

Unique in focusing on a single cuisine – or rather, on French cuisine, from Brittany to Provence – *Le Village Buffet* offers the most satisfying meal of any casino buffet. You'll find a wider array elsewhere, but if you're partial to French meat or fish, or simply fancy a fresh baguette and all the cheese you can eat, in a playful themed setting, don't miss it.

Restaurants

Beijing Noodle No. 9

MAP P.50, POCKET MAP F6
Caesars Palace, 3570 Las Vegas Blvd S ☎ 877 346 4642, ⓦ caesars.com/caesars-palace. Sun–Thurs 11am–12am, Fri & Sat 11am–2am.

Approached via aquariums that hold a thousand goldfish and resembling a pale, mysterious, underwater cavern, this Chinese noodle shop is one of Las Vegas's most enjoyable places to eat. Fortunately, the food matches the setting, though with dim sum buns and dumplings at around $13, and the (large) noodle dishes more like $20, so too do the prices.

Gordon Ramsay Pub & Grill

MAP P.50, POCKET MAP F6
Caesars Palace, 3570 Las Vegas Blvd S ☎ 702 731 7410, ⓦ caesars.com/caesars-palace. Mon–Thurs & Sun 11am–11pm, Fri & Sat 11am–midnight.

Stylized version of a British pub, run by TV chef and Las Vegas darling Gordon Ramsay, with some tables adjoining the casino floor and the rest inside, close to a bar decked out with pretend red phone kiosks. Fish and chips cost $30, steak-and-ale pies $26, while the many draught beers cost $9 during the "Hell's Kitchen" Happy Hour, weekdays 2–5pm.

Gordon Ramsay Steak

MAP P.50, POCKET MAP G7
Paris, 3655 Las Vegas Blvd S ☎ 877 346 4642, ⓦ caesars.com/paris-las-vegas. Daily 4.30–10.30pm.

For his first Las Vegas venture, perfectionist pottymouth Gordon Ramsay played it safe, opening a high-class steakhouse near Paris's main entrance – its tunnel approach represents the trip from France to England, incidentally. Diners select from a trolley laden with marbled, aged slabs of prime meat; a superbly cooked veal chop costs $55, a beef fillet $59 and the $150 tasting menu includes Beef Wellington.

Koi

MAP P.50, POCKET MAP G8
Planet Hollywood, 3667 Las Vegas Blvd S ☎ 702 454 4555, ⓦ koirestaurant.com. Mon–Thurs & Sun 5.30–10.30pm, Fri & Sat 5.30–11.30pm.

While not the celebrity favourite it is in Hollywood, this fancy restaurant serves tasty Japanese food at what, for Las Vegas, are reasonable prices – especially considering its views of Bellagio's fountains. Sushi rolls, tuna tartare or tempura shrimp cost well under $20, mains like steamed sea bass or wasabi short ribs up to $30.

Mesa Grill

MAP P.50, POCKET MAP F6
Caesars Palace, 3570 Las Vegas Blvd S
☎ 877 346 4642, ⓦ caesars.com. Mon–Fri
11am–2.30pm & 5–11pm, Sat & Sun
10.30am–3pm & 5–11pm.

Contemporary Southwestern
chef Bobby Flay, who made his
name in New York, has shown
enough commitment to his Las
Vegas outlet, across from the
Colosseum entrance, for it to
become Caesars' most dependable
fine-dining spot. Mexican-
influenced favourites include
sixteen-spice chicken, which costs
$18 in a lunch salad, more like
$33 for dinner.

Mon Ami Gabi

MAP P.50, POCKET MAP G7
Paris, 3655 Las Vegas Blvd S ☎ 702 944
4224, ⓦ monamigabi.com. Mon–Thurs
& Sun 7am–11pm, Fri & Sat 7am–midnight.

Among the first Las Vegas
restaurants to offer al fresco dining,
this exuberant evocation of a Paris
pavement brasserie remains the
city's premier lunchtime pick. For
a real taste of France, you can't beat
a $16 *croque-madame* (ham, cheese
and egg sandwich) for breakfast;
moules frites (mussels and chips) for
lunch ($14 or $26); or *steak frites*
for dinner ($30).

Nobu

MAP P.50, POCKET MAP F6
Caesars Palace, 3570 Las Vegas Blvd
S ☎ 702 785 6628, ⓦ caesars.com.
Mon–Thurs & Sun 5–11pm, Fri & Sat
5pm–midnight.

Flagship restaurant for the world-
spanning empire of Japanese-
Peruvian chef Nobu Matsuhisa,
whose fans are so devoted that
Caesars even has its own Nobu
hotel tower into the bargain.
Ambience and audience alike are
very upmarket; and the food is
exquisite, with hot mains including
black cod miso for $37 or beef
tenderloin for $36, and full chef's-
choice tasting menus starting
at $175.

The Palm

MAP P.50, POCKET MAP F5
Forum Shops, Caesars Palace ☎ 702
732 7256, ⓦ thepalm.com. Daily
11.30am–11pm.

A veteran of the Forum scene, this
offshoot of the legendary New
York steakhouse offers a stylish,
surprisingly formal escape from
the shopping mania outside.
For lunch, $18 will buy you a
salad, burger or sandwich. In the
evening, classic Italian veal dishes
cost $34–36, and a prime, 24oz
rib-eye steak is $59.

Yard House

MAP P.50, POCKET MAP H5
Linq Promenade, 3545 Las Vegas Blvd
S ☎ 702 597 0434, ⓦ yardhouse.com.
Mon–Thurs & Sun 11am–1am, Fri & Sat
11am–1.30am.

Lively restaurant/bar along the
pedestrian mall that leads to the
High Roller, where the extensive
food menu ranges from jambalaya
or Southern fried chicken to a
vegetarian quinoa salad, all priced
at well under $20. They also
offer craft ales and ciders from
around the world, many of which
you can indeed drink from a
genuine "yard".

Bars and lounges

Alto Bar

MAP P.50, POCKET MAP F6
Caesars Palace, 3570 Las Vegas Blvd
S ☎ 702 731 7778, ⓦ caesars.com/
caesars-palace. Sun–Thurs 10am–2am,
Fri–Sat 10pm–4am, live DJ Fri & Sat
9pm–4am.

Catch your breath after walking
Caesars' endless hallways in this
up-to-the-minute open-fronted
lounge, which replaced the much-
missed Seahorse Lounge in 2016.
Raised above the casino floor, and
specializing in very fancy cocktails
at $16–19 – a beer costs $9 – it's
the perfect spot to see and be seen,
though you can also hide away in a
private booth.

Mariah Carey at The Colosseum

Cleopatra's Barge

MAP P.50, POCKET MAP F6
Caesars Palace, 3570 Las Vegas Blvd S
📞 702 731 7333, Ⓦ caesars.com/caesars-palace. Tues–Thurs 7pm–2am, Fri & Sat 7pm–3am.
Caesars Palace was built just three years after Elizabeth Taylor's iconic performance as Cleopatra; centred on a floating replica of a Pharaonic barge, surrounded by gilded furniture and campy little nooks, this bar's been here ever since. A glorious reminder of Las Vegas's golden era, it never charges for admission, though every night sees appearances by either live musicians or DJs.

Napoleon Piano Bar

MAP P.50, POCKET MAP H7
Paris, 3655 Las Vegas Blvd S 📞 702 946 7000, Ⓦ caesars.com/paris-las-vegas.
Daily 5pm–1am. No cover charge.
Come in the early evening to this plush, dimly lit, bordello-red bar, poised halfway along the internal corridor that connects Paris to Bally's. While there may be a lounge act on stage, like a vocal group or comedian, it still feels like a sophisticated venue at which to enjoy a glass of champagne,

cognac, cocktails or cigars. Between 9pm and 1am nightly, however, things turn much more raucous, as duelling pianists vie to belt out whatever tunes the audience requests (and is prepared to tip for) – expect there to be energetic, enthusiastic sing-along renditions of *Bohemian Rhapsody* and the like.

Clubs and music venues

The Colosseum

MAP P.50, POCKET MAP F5
Caesars Palace, 3570 Las Vegas Blvd S
📞 866 227 5938, Ⓦ thecolosseum.com.
Showtimes and prices vary; Celine Dion typically ranges from $55–250.
Built in 2003 to house a long-term residency by Celine Dion, the 4000-seat Colosseum is the last great stronghold of the old-style Las Vegas headliner. Celine still returns frequently, while Rod Stewart and Mariah Carey also play regular extended engagements. Stars who appear for a night or two have included Jerry Seinfeld and Enrique Iglesias.

Absinthe

Drai's Beachclub & Nightclub

MAP P.50, POCKET MAP G7
The Cromwell, 3595 Las Vegas Blvd S
☏ 702 777 3800, Ⓦ caesars.com. Nightclub
Thurs–Sun 10.30pm–4am; Beach Club
summer only daily 11am–6pm. Cover $20.
This huge indoor-outdoor night/
day club, on The Cromwell's
roof, enjoys the best Strip views.
Named for EDM entrepreneur
and film producer Victor Drai,
previously responsible for creating
XS at Encore and Tryst at Wynn
Las Vegas, it has big-name DJs
and live performers – plus go-go
dancers, with poolside cabanas for
high-rollers.

Omnia

MAP P.50, POCKET MAP F6
Caesars Palace, 3570 Las Vegas Blvd S
☏ 702 785 6200, Ⓦ caesars.com. Tues &
Thurs–Sun 10.30pm–4am. Cover $20–50.
Unveiled in 2015 as the successor
to the massively popular Pure,
this club boasts a huge open-air
Strip-view terrace. Ordinary
mortals can expect a long queue,
and astonishing prices for drinks
($28 for a beer) for what is truly
a once-in-a-lifetime Las Vegas

experience, with the world's
biggest DJs.

Shows

Absinthe

MAP P.50, POCKET MAP F6
Caesars Palace, 3570 Las Vegas Blvd S
☏ 855 234 7469, Ⓦ caesars.com. Daily
8pm & 10pm. $109–199.
Staged in the round, in a marquee
on Caesars' outdoor Roman Plaza,
this no-holds-barred circus-tinged
burlesque show has taken Las Vegas
by storm. Conceived as a crude
and abrasive counterpoint to the
fey whimsy of Cirque du Soleil,
and eschewing PC in all its forms,
it's more of a drunken night out
than a traditional show, but it still
charges Cirque-level prices.

Big Elvis

MAP P.50, POCKET MAP G5
Piano Bar, Harrah's, 3475 Las Vegas Blvd S
☏ 702 369 5111, Ⓦ caesars.com/harrahs-
las-vegas. Mon, Wed & Fri 2–6pm. Free.
Las Vegas's biggest and best-loved
Elvis impersonator, Pete Vallee, has
shucked off the pounds in the last
few years to become merely Large

Elvis. His King-like voice still packs a powerful punch, though, and his mastery of Elvis's repertoire and easy audience rapport – requests welcome – make this the best free show in town.

Crazy Girls

MAP P.50, POCKET MAP G8
Planet Hollywood, 3667 Las Vegas Blvd S ☎ 702 777 2782, ⓦ caesars.com/planet-hollywood. Daily except Wed 9.30pm. $54–98. No under-21s.

Newly relocated from the sadly missed Riviera casino, the Strip's best-known "adult revue" remains a throwback to the Vegas of yesteryear. Half a dozen topless, if not exactly crazy, sequin-encrusted showgirls dance through a medley of show tunes, and there's an interlude of comedy and magic.

Donny & Marie

MAP P.50, POCKET MAP G6
Flamingo Las Vegas, 3555 Las Vegas Blvd S ☎ 702 777 2782, ⓦ caesars.com/flamingo-las-vegas. Tues–Sat 7.30pm. $104–250.

Anyone who doesn't need to ask the surname of this brother-and-sister duo will know what to expect – family-friendly service with a smile. As well as singing their combined hits, each does his or her own thing, and there's lots of new material, which in Donny's case includes a "hip-hop" routine. The old-style showroom seating is at shared tables, with drink service.

Gwen Stefani – Just A Girl

MAP P.50, POCKET MAP H9.
Planet Hollywood, Zappos Theater, 3667 Las Vegas Blvd S ☎ 855 234 7469, ⓦ caesars.com/planet-hollywood. Schedule varies seasonally. $80–$270.

Multi-platinum recording artist and global icon, Gwen Stefani, performs at Zappos Theater with her exclusive residency show, *Gwen Stefani – Just a Girl*. Zappos at Planet Hollywood is a 7000-seat state-of-the-art live entertainment venue.

Mac King

MAP P.50, POCKET MAP G5
Harrah's, 3475 Las Vegas Blvd S ☎ 702 693 6143, ⓦ mackingshow.com. Tues–Sat 1pm & 3pm. $38 & $49.

Just so there's no doubt, Mac King is billed as a comedy magician. With his clownish country-boy persona, clean-talking patter, easy way with his audience and family-friendly prices – plus of course his stunning sleight of hand – he's Las Vegas's best daytime entertainment bargain.

V – The Ultimate Variety Show

MAP P.50, POCKET MAP H8
Miracle Mile, Planet Hollywood, 3663 Las Vegas Blvd S ☎ 866 932 1818, ⓦ vtheshow.com. Daily 7pm & 8.30pm. $80 or $100.

This enjoyable, long-running Variety Show features established acts and crowd-pleasing routines. Regulars include "hip-hop contortionist" Turf; gloriously deadpan Mexican juggler Wally Eastwood; and Russ Merlin, whose Halloween mask audience-volunteer stunt brings the house down.

Donny & Marie

The North Strip

Along the North Strip a vibrant cluster of high-end properties compete to grab visitors' attention with gimmicks like volcanoes (the Mirage), Renaissance bridges (the Venetian) and all-round gilded opulence (Wynn Las Vegas). This part of the Strip is where things turn personal, with the giant casinos owned by fiercely competitive tycoons: specifically, Sheldon Adelson, owner of the Venetian and the Palazzo, is locked in fierce rivalry with Steve Wynn, of the similarly twinned Wynn Las Vegas and Encore. The North Strip was regarded as stretching almost all the way to downtown until the recession, when many of the veteran casinos that lay further north were closed down or blown up, and most of the projects scheduled to replace them abandoned. However, change is afoot as investors are beginning to be lured back.

The Mirage

MAP P.64, POCKET MAP F4
3400 Las Vegas Blvd S ☎ 702 791 7111,
Ⓦ mirage.com.

Unveiled as entrepreneur Steve Wynn's first Strip venture, in 1989 – when Las Vegas seemed to be in decline, and no new Strip hotels had been built for sixteen years – the **Mirage** can justly claim to have changed the city overnight. Proving that by investing in luxury, glamour and spectacle, casinos could bring back the crowds, it spawned such a host of imitators that now, ironically, it no longer stands out from the pack. Following endless mergers and buy outs, it now belongs to MGM Resorts, which tends to concentrate its attention on its string of properties further south, while Wynn has built his latest resort, Wynn Las Vegas (see page 66), and adjoining Encore, a short way north.

There's still plenty to like about the Mirage, from its **glassed-in atrium**, complete with towering tropical trees, via its well-judged array of restaurants and bars, to its huge complex of pools and gardens, part of which is home to the **Secret Garden and Dolphin Habitat**. It's also still at the top of the entertainment tree, having replaced uber-camp German magicians Siegfried and Roy with the Beatles showcase, *Love* (see page 76) and amazing impressionist Terry Fator (see page 76).

Steve Wynn's most radical innovation was to target the Mirage at pedestrians wandering the Strip in search of things to do. Hence the artificial **volcano** outside, which erupts at hourly intervals, usually from 8pm to 10pm.

Secret Garden and Dolphin Habitat

MAP P.64, POCKET MAP E4
Mirage, 3400 Las Vegas Blvd S ☎ 702 791 7188, Ⓦ miragehabitat.com. Daily 10am–7pm. Adults $22, ages 4–12 $17.

Although a wayward tiger sadly curtailed the performing careers of Siegfried and Roy in 2003, the menagerie of big cats that featured in their magic is still here. Cages in the **Secret Garden and Dolphin Habitat** contain big cats such as black leopards, golden tigers and their signature white lions and tigers. There are also two pools of bottlenose dolphins, which interact with visitors.

TI (Treasure Island)

MAP P.64, POCKET MAP G3
3300 Las Vegas Blvd S ☎ 702 894 7111, ⓦ treasureisland.com.

TI (Treasure Island) was built in 1993 as a sort of kid brother to the Mirage (see page 62) next door, with an all-pervasive pirate theme aimed at family visitors. While it's still physically connected to the Mirage by a free **monorail**, it's now under separate ownership, and distances itself from its yo-ho-ho past by using the anodyne acronym TI.

The most prominent feature of Treasure Island during its first twenty years was the shallow **lagoon** in front, home to twin replica pirate ships that were crewed first by battling buccaneers and then later by gyrating, bikini-clad "sirens" whose after-dark music-and-dance shows lured in vast crowds. Architectural theorists tied themselves in knots arguing whether Treasure Island was a building, a performance space or a theme park. Ships and sirens alike have now gone, prosaically replaced by a crass Mexican "party restaurant", *Señor Frog's*, and a huge CVS grocery/pharmacy.

Phil Ruffin, former owner of the now-vanished New Frontier, bought TI in 2008, when MGM Resorts ran short of cash to build CityCenter. He's steadily turning it into a blue-collar joint, home to nightspots like *Gilley's Saloon* (see page 74), though he's hung on to Cirque's first-ever Las Vegas show, *Mystère* (see page 76).

The Venetian

MAP P.64, POCKET MAP G4
3355 Las Vegas Blvd S ☎ 702 414 1000, ⓦ venetian.com.

The hugely successful **Venetian** casino opened in 1999 on the site of the much-mourned Sands, the former Las Vegas home of Frank Sinatra and the Rat Pack. Even if its owner, Sheldon Adelson, may lack the design flair of Steve Wynn, he has an unarguable genius for making money. After buying the Sands in 1988, he amassed a billion-dollar fortune from the annual tech-industry trade show COMDEX

The Mirage

Chapel of the Flowers (0.5 mile) & △ A Little White Wedding Chapel (1.5 miles)

BUFFETS
The Buffet at Wynn   4
Cravings   13

RESTAURANTS
Bouchon   12
(in Venezia Tower, Level 10)
Delmonico   9
Grand Lux Cafe   6
Lavo Italian Restaurant
 & Lounge   7
LVB Burgers   15
Pantry   14
Pho   8
Red 8   5
Sinatra   2
Tao Asian Bistro   10
(on Second Level)
Top of the World   1
(on 106th floor)
Wazuzu   3
Yardbird Southern
 Table & Bar   11
(on Second Level)

SHOPS
Bonanza Gifts   1
Encore Esplanade   2
Fashion Show   4
Grand Canal Shoppes   6
(on Second Level)
Shoppes at the Palazzo   5
(on Second Level)
Wynn Esplanade   3

BARS & LOUNGES
Gilley's Saloon   6
OTORO   9
Parasol Up,
 Parasol Down   4
Peppermill
 Fireside Lounge   1
Señor Frog's   5

**CLUBS &
MUSIC VENUES**
1 OAK   8
Encore Beach Club   2
Tao (on Second Level)   7
XS   3

SHOWS
Human Nature Jukebox   3
Le Rêve   1
Love   5
Mystère   2
Terry Fator   4

0   metres   500
0   yards   500

Stratosphere Tower
& Thrill Rides

THE STRATOSPHERE

Chapel of
the Bells

SLS LAS VEGAS

SLS STATION

WESTGATE LAS VEGAS STATION

WESTGATE LAS VEGAS RESORT
(formerly Las Vegas Hilton)

Las Vegas Convention Center

Splash Zone

CIRCUS CIRCUS

The Adventuredome

Midway
(2nd floor)

Former site of The Riviera

Guardian Angel Cathedral

TRUMP INTERNATIONAL HOTEL

ENCORE

Wynn Golf Course

Fashion Show

Lake of Dreams

WYNN LAS VEGAS

TI (TREASURE ISLAND)

THE PALAZZO

THE VENETIAN

Sands Convention Center

Grand Canal

Volcano

Madame Tussauds

THE MIRAGE

HARRAH'S

Secret Garden and Dolphin Habitat

The Forum

HARRAH'S/THE LINQ STATION

Las Vegas High Roller

THE LINQ

The North Strip

Another one bites the dust

Yet another veteran fixture vanished from the Strip skyline in 2016, with the controlled explosion of the Riviera's one surviving tower, a year on from the casino finally closing its doors after six decades. When built in 1955, by a consortium ranging from mobsters to the Marx Brothers, it was the Strip's first high-rise resort, designed to evoke French Mediterranean glamour. With nine storeys, it was also home to the Strip's first elevator.

During the last decade or so, as neighbours like the Stardust, the Westward Ho, and Silver City were, one by one, blasted into oblivion, the Riviera's neon starburst facade had remained a welcome flash of colour on the North Strip. It was always a losing battle, though, and it's a sign of the times that it was ultimately purchased not by a casino operator, but by the Las Vegas Convention & Visitors Authority, which paid a reported $182.5 million to make room for a proposed expansion of the city's **Convention Center**. Resorts World Las Vegas, a mutibilion-dollar, Chinese-themed casino is being built on the old site of Stardust. Construction is in full swing for the complex's three hotels and multiple Chinese restaurants.

and has more recently expanded his casino operations into Macau, as well as ploughing huge sums into conservative politics at home.

The Venetian itself is a re-creation of the ultimate honeymoon photo album; Adelson returned from his 1991 honeymoon trip to Venice with the idea of building a vast replica of the city. Around a dozen distinct Venetian landmarks squeeze side by side into the casino's Strip facade, while its main entrance lies between a pair brought to Venice's Piazza San Marco from Constantinople in 1172. One is topped by St Theodore, the city's original patron, the other by a winged lion representing St Mark, who became its patron in 1204.

The interior of the Venetian holds fewer specific echoes of the city. While it's the **Grand Canal** upstairs that draws in the sightseers, it's the sheer opulence elsewhere, from the huge staircases and resplendent frescoes to the endless hallways of marble tiles, which makes this the most impressive public space on the Strip. It's also among the busiest, thanks to an excellent crop of restaurants, shops and theatres, and the Sands Convention Center at the back.

When it first opened, the Venetian out-trumped Bellagio's Gallery of Fine Art (see page 43) by opening two separate Guggenheim art museums. Both have long since disappeared, but the exhibition space near the hotel lobby is still used for occasional temporary art shows.

The Grand Canal

MAP P.64, POCKET MAP G4 & K5
Venetian, 3355 Las Vegas Blvd S ☎ 702 414 4300, Ⓦ venetian.com. Gondola rides indoors Mon–Thurs & Sun 10am–11pm, Fri & Sat 10am–midnight; outdoors Sun–Thurs 5–10.45pm, Fri & Sat 5–11.45pm. $29, $116 for a two-person private ride.
You can't have Venice without the **Grand Canal**. The Venetian has it twice – outdoors beside the Strip and as the centrepiece of its shopping and dining mall upstairs. While neither section is particularly large, let alone authentic, you have to admire the sheer nerve. With its artificial sky,

the indoor segment is obviously modelled on the Forum and features a large plaza based on St Mark's Square. Singing gondoliers take paying customers on short gondola rides along the canal.

Madame Tussauds

MAP P.64, POCKET MAP G4
Venetian, 3377 Las Vegas Blvd S ☎ 702 860 7805, Ⓦ madametussauds.com. Mon–Thurs & Sun 10am–9pm, Fri & Sat 10am–10pm. $30, ages 7–12 $20; twenty percent discount online.

Entered directly from the Strip, just off the Venetian's attractive covered Rialto Bridge, **Madame Tussauds** taps into Las Vegas's craving for close celebrity contact by allowing visitors to get personal with waxworks ranging from Brad Pitt and Daniel Craig to the bizarre body-painted Blue Men (even though they're not actually recognizable as individuals). With the single exception of the President in the White House, for whom there's an extra fee, you're free to take unlimited photos of, and with, all of your friendly, new-found waxy playmates.

Madame Tussauds

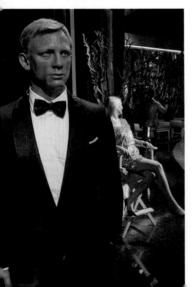

The Palazzo

MAP P.64, POCKET MAP H3
3325 Las Vegas Blvd S ☎ 866 263 3001, Ⓦ palazzo.com.

Even if owner Sheldon Adelson insists that his **Palazzo** resort is entirely separate from the Venetian next door, no one takes the distinction seriously; broad internal walkways enable visitors to step from one property to the other and barely notice the transition. Counted as a single unit, this would be, with over seven thousand rooms, the largest hotel in the world.

Considered on its own, on the other hand, the Palazzo is among the least interesting casinos in Las Vegas. As well as its own very high-end shopping mall and a decent crop of restaurants, it's home to the *Lavo* nightclub/restaurant, but has nothing of any interest for casual sightseers. Even the giant butterflies added to jazz up its central waterfall feature look more like one of rival Steve Wynn's cast-off ideas than anything truly original.

Wynn Las Vegas

MAP P.64, POCKET MAP J2
3131 Las Vegas Blvd S ☎ 702 770 7000, Ⓦ wynnlasvegas.com.

Steve Wynn, the man who's credited with inventing the new Las Vegas by opening first the Mirage and then Bellagio, bounced back from losing control of the Mirage organization by building his own self-named resort, **Wynn Las Vegas**, in 2005. Like his great rival at the Venetian-Palazzo next door, Sheldon Adelson, Wynn swiftly complemented Wynn Las Vegas with Encore, and now runs two nominally distinct resorts on the same site.

When Wynn bought this prime slice of real estate it held the fabled *Desert Inn*, where Howard Hughes lived out his final years in paranoid seclusion. Steve Wynn doesn't do secondhand, though; he blew the whole place up and set to work building bigger and better than ever. The result, a majestic bronze crescent soaring skywards alongside the similar Encore, is breathtaking. Rendered almost blind by a degenerative eye disease, Wynn loves to fill his casinos with vibrant, dazzling swathes of colour – hence the plush red carpets that sweep through the interior, leading to a flower-packed **central garden** where the trees are bedecked with fairy lights and lanterns.

Because Steve Wynn wanted every Las Vegas visitor to come and admire Bellagio and the Mirage, he gave them all sorts of crowd-pleasing novelties. Wynn Las Vegas, being targeted more exclusively at the luxury end of the market with its array of consistently high-end restaurants and nightspots, holds fewer specific attractions and is therefore not quite so much of a must-see. Its most unusual feature is the **Lake of Dreams**, an expanse of water illuminated at night with changing projections, and peopled by mysterious mannequins. Unlike the Mirage's volcano, it was deliberately designed to only be visible to visitors from inside the property.

Encore

MAP P.64, POCKET MAP J1
3121 Las Vegas Blvd S ☎ 702 770 7000, ⓦ wynnlasvegas.com.

Encore stands in the same relation to Wynn Las Vegas as does the Palazzo to the Venetian. Erected three years after its elder brother, in 2008, and joined to it seamlessly via plush corridors, it's every bit as lavish – this is where Prince Harry was photographed naked in 2012 – but offers little sense of identity in its own right. In a deliberate piece of provocative one-upmanship, Steve Wynn built it 11ft taller than rival Sheldon Adelson's Palazzo, unveiled earlier the same year. Adelson, it's widely believed, responded by opening a large, downmarket Walgreens pharmacy at the Palazzo's Strip-level corner, thumbing his nose at the pretentious shops preferred by Wynn.

Like all Wynn's properties, Encore is ablaze with colour, like an episode of *Sesame Street* that's brought to you by the colour Red and the insects Butterfly and Dragonfly. Other than the general air of luxury, its main strategy to bring in visitors is via entertainment.

The indoor-outdoor, day-night **Encore Beach Club** (see page 75) has been a huge hit, not least with visiting British royalty, while Steve Wynn pulled off a genuine coup by luring country superstar Garth Brooks out of retirement for a long-term deal. Brooks has now moved on, but Wynn has plenty more up his sleeve, including turning the golf course out the back into a giant tropical oasis.

Guardian Angel Cathedral

MAP P.64, POCKET MAP K1
302 Cathedral Way ☎ 702 735 5241, ⓦ gaclv.org. Masses Mon–Fri 8am & 12.10pm, Sat 2.30pm, 4pm & 5.30pm, Sun 8am, 9.30am, 11am, 12.30pm & 5pm.
Of all the Strip's eye-catching architectural wonders, perhaps the most unexpected stands just north of Encore – the Roman Catholic **Guardian Angel Cathedral**. It was built in 1963, on land donated by the former owner of both the Desert Inn and Stardust casinos, Moe Dalitz, a Jewish gangster from Detroit. Seeking to improve his public image, he paid modernist architect Paul Revere Williams to design this sloping tent-like structure. A stained-glass window to the right of the altar serves as a memorial to the Strip as it looked in the 1960s, depicting long-gone casinos like the Sands, the Stardust and the International.

Circus Circus

MAP P.64, POCKET MAP K8
2880 Las Vegas Blvd S ☎ 702 734 0410, ⓦ circuscircus.com.
Guarded by the giant figure of Lucky the Clown – if you suffer from coulrophobia, or fear of

The Adventuredome

clowns, you won't like Lucky one bit – the candy-striped big top of **Circus Circus** has loomed beside the Strip for half a century. However, despite being owned by MGM Resorts, Circus Circus was battered and isolated by the recession. Former neighbours including the New Frontier and the Stardust have disappeared, while few of the fancy new developments that were supposed to replace them ever materialized – the Fontainebleau Las Vegas was constructed but never opened, while ambitious plans to build first Echelon (2008–2014), and subsequently the Asian-themed Resorts World (2014–2016), which was purportedly going to feature live pandas, came to nothing. Pedestrian traffic hereabouts has dwindled to nothing, to leave Circus Circus cut off from the Strip in general, and from MGM Resorts' other properties in particular.

Circus Circus has always been a strange, unsettling hybrid of circus and casino. It famously attracted the scorn of Hunter S. Thompson, who wrote in *Fear and Loathing in Las Vegas* that "Circus Circus is what the whole hep world would be doing on Saturday night if the Nazis had won the war". When it opened, in 1968, as Jay Sarno's attempt to repeat his success with Caesars Palace, it didn't include any hotel rooms and charged customers an entry fee. At first it was very much an adult playground, reflecting the sleazier side of carnival attractions. It took a few years to hit on the formula it still follows, of catering largely to families by offering **live circus acts** and other child-oriented attractions. Coupled with its low room rates, the result has been that Circus Circus has become the tackiest of the major Strip casinos.

Circus Circus is so huge that it's the only Strip casino to have an internal **monorail system**, to take guests to their rooms. With its low ceilings and endless corridors, lined with fast-food outlets and novelty stores, it's quite a maze, and it can be hard to find the mezzanine area that's home to the **Midway**. The circular stage here plays host to a constant succession of free circus acts, from trapeze artists and jugglers to tightrope walkers and, yes, clowns. Old-fashioned sideshows offer kids the chance to kick-start a lifetime's gambling habit by winning stuffed toys. They'll also love Splash Zone, Vegas's newest water park, with its water playground and thrilling slides.

The Adventuredome

MAP P.64, POCKET MAP J8
Circus Circus, 2880 Las Vegas Blvd S
☎ 702 794 3939, ⓦ circuscircus.com. Daily 10am–midnight during school holidays, otherwise Mon–Thurs & Sun 10am–9pm, Fri & Sat 10am–midnight. $6–12 individual

attractions, $33 all-day wristband, children under 4ft $18.

Las Vegas's largest theme park, the **Adventuredome**, is housed in a giant pink enclosure at the back of Circus Circus, a long walk from the Strip. Entirely indoors and on a much smaller scale than, say, Disney World or Universal Studios, it's aimed very much at children. Adults may well enjoy the twisting, looping **Canyon Blaster** and the even more ferocious, ultra-steep **El Loco**, but most of the space is given over to SpongeBob Squarepants simulator rides and the like.

SLS Las Vegas

MAP P.64, POCKET MAP L2
2535 Las Vegas Blvd S ☎ 702 761 7000, Ⓦ slslasvegas.com.

The veteran Sahara, a Strip fixture since 1952, fell victim to the recession and closed its doors in 2011. It was not actually demolished, though, simply stripped of its former *Arabian Nights* minarets and comedy camels, and given a glossy new facade plus an injection of Philippe Starck stylings, to reopen in 2014 as **SLS Las Vegas**.

Calling itself a "boutique resort" despite having three hotel towers and over 1600 rooms, SLS is part of a rapidly expanding nightlife and hotel chain with outlets in Beverley Hills, South Beach and New York. An entertainment-based property pitched a rung or two below the Strip's top tier, it's home to an indoor-outdoor pool and nightclub, *Foxtail*, plus big-name restaurants including *Bazaar Meat* and the Starck-designed sushi place *Katsuya*.

The vast empty lot across the Strip from SLS belongs to MGM Resorts. Despite sustaining huge losses when they staged the US version of the Rock in Rio festival here in 2015, they hope to use the site for future events.

The Stratosphere

MAP P.64, POCKET MAP L2
2000 Las Vegas Blvd S ☎ 702 380 7777, Ⓦ stratospherehotel.com. Tower Mon–Thurs & Sun 10am–1am, Fri & Sat 10am–2am. $20, discounts for guests.

At 1149ft, the **Stratosphere** makes a conveniently colossal landmark to denote the northern limit of the Strip, even if strictly speaking it's located in the city proper, a full mile north of Circus Circus, its nearest active neighbour. It took quite a feat of engineering to build the tallest structure west of the Mississippi in the shifting sands of Nevada; amazingly, its foundations are a mere 12ft deep.

Served by Deuce buses, but not the city's Monorail system, the Stratosphere holds nothing for sightseers apart from the **Stratosphere Tower** itself. Two observation decks, one outdoors at the very summit and the other indoors on the floor below, offer fabulous views over the city and hold fascinating displays explaining everything you can see. Most visitors are up here strictly for kicks, however, to dice with death on the array of **Thrill Rides** at the very top.

Stratosphere Thrill Rides

MAP P.64, POCKET MAP L2
Stratosphere, 2000 Las Vegas Blvd S ☎ 702 380 7711, Ⓦ stratospherehotel.com. Mon–Thurs & Sun 11am–1am, Fri & Sat 11am–2am. X-Scream, Big Shot & Insanity: one ride (inc tower) $25, two $30, three $35, unlimited rides $40, SkyJump $120, minimum age 14.

The top of the Stratosphere serves as the launching point for several terrifying **thrill rides**, for daredevils only. **X-Scream** is a sort of giant boat that tips upside down a thousand feet above the Strip; **Insanity** is a crane that spins riders out over the abyss; **Big Shot** is a glorified sofa that free falls a couple of hundred feet. Worst of all is the **SkyJump**, in which harnessed jumpers step off a platform to fall 855ft.

Shops

Bonanza Gifts

MAP P.64, POCKET MAP L3
2440 Las Vegas Blvd S ☎ 702 385 7359,
Ⓦ worldslargestgiftshop.com. Daily
8am–12am.

The self-proclaimed "World's Largest Gift Shop", where Sahara Avenue meets the Strip, is *the* place to buy Las Vegas souvenirs. Trinkets celebrating the city, old and new, include countless variations on the iconic "Welcome to Fabulous Las Vegas" sign and memorabilia from individual casinos, such as packs of used playing cards.

Fashion Show

MAP P.64, POCKET MAP G2
3200 Las Vegas Blvd S ☎ 702 369
8382, Ⓦ thefashionshow.com. Mon–Sat
10am–9pm, Sun 11am–7pm.

The only stand-alone shopping mall on the Strip, and for most Las Vegas visitors the only serious rival to in-casino malls such as the Forum, the Fashion Show spreads through two two-storey buildings across from Wynn Las Vegas. Despite the eye-catching circular sculpture that dangles over the pavement, it's in no sense an attraction, simply a functional shopping destination. Unlike its Strip rivals, it's large enough to hold department stores including Macy's, Sak's Fifth Avenue, Nordstrom and Dillard's, as well as an Apple Store and the usual clothing chains.

Grand Canal Shoppes

MAP P.64, POCKET MAP K5
Second Level, Venetian, 3377 Las
Vegas Blvd S ☎ 702 414 4525,
Ⓦ thegrandcanalshoppes.com. Mon–Thurs
& Sun 10am–11pm, Fri & Sat 10am–
midnight.

Arrayed along the waterfront upstairs in the Venetian, the Grand Canal Shoppes may surpass Caesars' Forum for sheer chutzpah, but as a shopping destination the mall is not a serious match. It does hold a handful of clothing chains, such as Hugo Boss, but consists largely of souvenir and impulse-purchase stores, with a big emphasis on showy jewellery. After all, this was where Michael Jackson went on the celebrated million-dollar shopping spree that's recorded in Martin Bashir's 2003 TV documentary about the star.

Shoppes at the Palazzo

MAP P.64, POCKET MAP K5
Second Level, Palazzo, 3325 Las
Vegas Blvd S ☎ 702 414 4525,
Ⓦ thegrandcanalshoppes.com. Mon–Thurs
& Sun 10am–11pm, Fri & Sat 10am–
midnight.

More in keeping with the smart stores of Wynn Las Vegas next door than the gimmicky tone of the nearby Grand Canal, the Shoppes at the Palazzo are scattered around the resort's second floor. Few casual visitors pass this way, so the atmosphere tends to be hushed. Exclusive fashion boutiques include Jimmy Choo and Diane von Furstenberg, and there are also several expensive jewellery outlets.

Wynn and Encore Esplanades

MAP P.64, POCKET MAP H2 & J1
Wynn Las Vegas, 3131 Las Vegas Blvd S
☎ 702 770 7000, Ⓦ wynnlasvegas.com.
Mon–Thurs 10am–11pm, Fri & Sat 10am–
midnight.

There's a separate esplanade of shops in both Wynn Las Vegas and Encore, though they're all but identical in their high-end opulence. For ordinary mortals, fashion boutiques like Alexander McQueen, Givenchy and Chloé, and watch stores such as Jaeger-LeCoultre and IWC Schaffhausen, make great window shopping.

Buffets

The Buffet at Wynn

MAP P.64, POCKET MAP J2

Wynn Las Vegas, 3131 Las Vegas Blvd S ⊕ 702 770 7000, ⓦ wynnlasvegas.com. Daily brunch 7.30am–3.30pm $29; dinner 3.30–9.30pm, Mon–Thurs $43, Fri–Sun $60. Buffet and show packages from $95 to $130.

Buffets are always a high priority for Steve Wynn and at Wynn Las Vegas he's got one of the best buffets in town. In a plush room that oozes belle epoque excess, this is buffet food at its finest, with dishes from lamb osso bucco and smoked duck salad to scallop ceviche and sushi rolls. While serious foodies will always prefer a real restaurant, if you've got a large appetite or are in a group with varying tastes, you won't be disappointed. About $53 per head.

Cravings

MAP P.64, POCKET MAP F4
Mirage, 3400 Las Vegas Blvd S ⊕ 702 791 7111, ⓦ mirage.com. Breakfast daily 7–11am $19; lunch daily 11am–3pm $24; dinner Mon–Thurs 3–9pm $30; dinner Fri–Sun 3–9pm $33; brunch Sat & Sun 8am–3pm $29.

With its contemporary design aesthetic – rare indeed for a Las Vegas buffet, and resembling

some futuristic space-age diner – *Cravings* is on a smaller scale than most of its rivals. Where possible, dishes such as stir-fries or omelettes are cooked to order; others are beautifully presented on gleaming platters. This is still mass catering – but it's a good option for a quick meal.

Restaurants

Bouchon

MAP P.64, POCKET MAP H4
Level 10, Venezia Tower, Venetian, 3355 Las Vegas Blvd S ⊕ 702 414 6200, ⓦ venetian. com. Breakfast Mon–Thurs 7am–1pm; brunch Fri–Sun 7am–2pm; dinner nightly 5–10pm; oyster bar daily 3–10pm.

Thomas Keller's scrupulous evocation of a French bistro, hidden away on the tenth floor of the Venetian's Venezia tower, may not have novelty value, but it's a lovely, relaxed spot, with plentiful outdoor seating and food that's nothing short of *magnifique*. Brunch is the best value, with sandwiches or quiche for around $20; dinner mains like *steak frites* or *sole meunière* cost $38.

Bouchon

Delmonico

MAP P.64, POCKET MAP H3
Casino Level, Venetian, 3355 Las Vegas
Blvd S ☎ 702 414 3737, ⓦ venetian.
com. Mon–Thurs & Sun 11.30am–2pm
& 5–10pm, Fri & Sat 11.30am–2pm &
5–10.30pm.

Renowned for bringing New
Orleans food to the nation,
chef Emeril Lagasse has made
the Venetian the setting for a
sophisticated steakhouse with
a strong contemporary flavour.
While the lunch menu centres on
salads ($12–17) and sandwiches
($20), the big guns come out
in the evening, with giant juicy
steaks (from $55) and starters like
barbecue shrimp ($20).

Grand Lux Cafe

MAP P.64, POCKET MAP H3
Casino Level, Palazzo, 3325 Las Vegas
Blvd S ☎ 702 414 3888, ⓦ venetian.com.
Open 24hr.

Although it's owned by the
Cheesecake Factory chain, and has
itself gone national, the *Grand Lux
Cafe* was originally created as a
casual, but nonetheless classy, 24-
hour coffee shop for the Venetian,
and swiftly added this slightly
smarter branch in the Palazzo.
Both offer wide-ranging menus of

Wazuzu

fresh, well-prepared favourites from
around the world at good prices –
pizza and salad costs $14, Salisbury
steak $17, or Cajun shrimp and
chicken jambalaya $20 – and have
their own on-site bakeries.

Lavo Italian Restaurant & Lounge

MAP P.64, POCKET MAP H3
Casino Level, Palazzo, 3325 Las Vegas Blvd
S ☎ 702 791 1800, ⓦ lavolv.com. Mon–Sun
5–11pm, Sat 10am–2pm, Sun 10am–4pm.

Considering it's attached to the
exclusive *Lavo* nightclub, this is an
oddly traditional Italian restaurant,
dark and romantic rather than
loud or brash. The food too is
rich and authentic, and the prices
relatively restrained, with pizzas
for $22, pasta specials a little more
and Mediterranean classics like veal
parmigiano costing up to $46.

LVB Burgers

MAP P.64, POCKET MAP F5
Mirage, 3400 Las Vegas Blvd S ☎ 702 792
7888, ⓦ mirage.com. Mon–Thurs & Sun
11am–12am, Fri & Sat 11am–2am.

So-called "gourmet burger" joints
are all the rage in Las Vegas. Lively
long after midnight, this one, in
a former tiger pen near the front
of the Mirage, serves a delicious
blue cheese burger for $16, an Old
School burger for $15, or a $17
Brewster Island fish burger.

Pantry

MAP P.64, POCKET MAP F4
Mirage, 3400 Las Vegas Blvd S ☎ 702 696
7050, ⓦ mirage.com. Daily 24hr.

Located at the heart of the
Mirage by the guest elevators.
Serves wholesome favourites
such as soups, salads and loaded
sandwiches, with breakfast available
round-the-clock for your fix of
fluffy pancakes, omelettes and
scrambled eggs.

Pho

MAP P.64, POCKET MAP G3
TI, 3300 Las Vegas Blvd S ☎ 800 944 7444,
ⓦ treasureisland.com. Mon–Thurs & Sun

11am–11.30pm, Fri & Sat 11am–2am. You could easily fail to notice that half the time, half of TI's 24-hour *Coffee Shop* is given over to this inexpensive and excellent Vietnamese diner. The pho of the name is steaming noodle soup; prices start at $16 and increase depending on the meat or fish you add. They also serve spring rolls and dry noodle dishes, and sneak in some sushi options and Chinese favourites too.

Red 8

MAP P.64, POCKET MAP J2
Wynn Las Vegas, 3131 Las Vegas Blvd S
☎ 702 770 3380, ⓦ wynnlasvegas.com.
Mon–Thurs & Sun 11.30am–midnight, Fri &
Sat 11.30am–1am.

This decadent, deep-red, pan-Asian restaurant makes a stylish retreat from Wynn's adjoining casino floor and serves a full menu of Chinese classics, from dim sum dumplings at $10 to chow mein or *ho fun* noodles for around $20, as well as Thai fish cakes and Malaysian satay and *laksa*.

Sinatra

MAP P.64, POCKET MAP J1
Encore, 3121 Las Vegas Blvd S ☎ 702
770 5320, ⓦ wynnlasvegas.com. Daily
5.30–10pm.

The Sinatra name, licensed by Frank's family, is of course a gimmick, but it tells you what to expect – the kind of idealized Italian restaurant the Rat Pack might have frequented back in the 1960s, formal and romantic and not in the slightest bit calorie-conscious. Ol' Blue Eyes is everywhere, from the speakers to the menu, with his favourite spaghetti and clams for $35 and osso bucco "My Way" for $54.

Tao Asian Bistro

MAP P.64, POCKET MAP J5
Second Level, The Venetian, 3355 Las Vegas
Blvd S ☎ 702 388 8338, ⓦ venetian.com.
Mon–Thurs & Sun 5pm–midnight, Fri & Sat
5pm–1am.

By far the busiest and most profitable restaurant in the entire US, *Tao* is a place to come for the experience – the over-the-top opium-den decor, the giant Buddha statue, the crowds of dressed-up clubbers getting ready to party in the *Tao* nightclub next door – as much as the showy Asian food. And the food is good – pork or duck with sizzling fried rice costs $15, and steak or sea bass is around $38.

Top of the World

MAP P.64, POCKET MAP L2
Stratosphere, 2000 Las Vegas Blvd S
☎ 702 380 7711, ⓦ topoftheworldlv.
com. Lunch and dinner Mon–Thurs & Sun
11am–10.30pm, Fri & Sat 11am–11pm.

While it's a lot classier than the hotel-casino far below, this restaurant only stands out for the compelling reason that it's over 800ft up in the air, and revolves every 80 minutes to give magnificent views over the Strip. Lunchtime is the cheapest time (sandwiches from $25; steaks $34), but dinner is much more romantic (mains start at $40).

Wazuzu

MAP P.64, POCKET MAP J1
Encore, 3121 Las Vegas Blvd S ☎ 702 770
5388, ⓦ wynnlasvegas.com. Mon–Thurs
& Sun 11.30am–10.30pm, Fri & Sat
11.30am–1am.

Approached by an avenue of six colossal gilt pears, and featuring a huge crystal dragon squirming along its back wall, *Wazuzu* is by far the best-looking restaurant in Encore, and it serves the best food too. As well as sushi, it draws on Asian cuisines from Japan (seaweed salad $8) and Mongolia (wok-tossed beef $23) to Thailand (chicken basil stir-fry $23). Be sure to try the *sake* too.

Yardbird Southern Table & Bar

MAP P.64, POCKET MAP K5
The Venetian, 3355 Las Vegas Blvd S ☎ 702
297 6541, ⓦ venetian.com. Lunch Mon–Fri
11am–4pm; dinner Sun–Thurs 4–11pm,
Fri & Sat 4pm–12am; brunch Sat & Sun
10am–4pm.

Classic Southern cooking, culture and hospitality. Lunch menu includes fresh sandwiches and salads for around $14. Supper is all about big flavours and comfort food, such as shrimp n' grits for $28 and peppered gnocchi pot pie, $21.

Bars and lounges

Gilley's Saloon

MAP P.64, POCKET MAP G3
TI, 3300 Las Vegas Blvd S ☎ 702 894 7111, Ⓦ gilleyslasvegas.com. Mon–Thurs & Sun 11am–2am, Fri & Sat 11am–4am. $10 cover for live bands.

This lively country and rodeo saloon practically defines the new TI. Bikini-clad "Gilley Girls" ride the mechanical bulls, and you can join a free line-dancing lesson most nights at 7pm, drink two-for-one rum cocktails until 10pm, or dance to honky-tonk bands until long after midnight.

OTORO

MAP P.64, POCKET MAP F4
Mirage, 3400 Las Vegas Blvd S ☎ 866 339 4566, Ⓦ mirage.com. Mon–Thurs & Sun 5.30–9.30pm, Fri & Sat 5pm–10pm.

While the dining room of OTORO, at the heart of the Mirage, serves everything from steak to sushi, the separate lounge and bar area is a stunning, glamorous spot for pre- or after-show drinks, swathed in flowing, spotlit fabrics and offering surprisingly intimate seating areas.

Parasol Up, Parasol Down

MAP P.64, POCKET MAP J2
Wynn Las Vegas, 3131 Las Vegas Blvd S ☎ 702 770 7000, Ⓦ wynnlasvegas.com. Mon–Thurs & Sun 11am–3am, Fri & Sat 11am–4am.

A quintessential example of the Wynn way with design, these twin upstairs-downstairs bars, festooned with richly coloured umbrellas and filling Wynn's central stairway, are the perfect place to admire the Lake of Dreams. A cocktail or two,

and you'll feel right at Las Vegas's absurd and exhilarating heart.

Peppermill Fireside Lounge

MAP P.64, POCKET MAP B11
2985 Las Vegas Blvd S ☎ 702 735 4177, Ⓦ peppermilllasvegas.com. Daily 24hr.

A magnificent relic from the glory days, somehow surviving on the North Strip just north of Encore, this wonderful Vegas veteran outclasses any of the casino lounges with its pink neon, mirrored walls and central flame-spouting fire pit, and a spectacular assortment of colourful cocktails, culminating in its signature 64oz Scorpion. The attached diner serves an appropriately retro-flavoured food menu, from ham-and-egg breakfasts to pineapple-topped burgers and dinner steaks.

Señor Frog's

MAP P.64, POCKET MAP G3
TI, 3300 Las Vegas Blvd S ☎ 702 337 7577, Ⓦ senorfrogs.com. Daily from 12pm.

This totally raucous, hugely enjoyable indoor-outdoor Mexican-themed bar overlooks what used to be the pirate lagoon outside Treasure Island, and with its enormous open-air deck it makes a great spot for a sunset margarita or after-hours cocktail. As well as live bands on Fridays, they have a drag brunch every Saturday, followed by a Latin night.

Clubs and music venues

1 OAK

MAP P.64, POCKET MAP F4
Mirage, 3400 Las Vegas Blvd S ☎ 702 693 8300, Ⓦ 1oaklasvegas.com. Wed, Fri & Sat 10.30pm–4am. Cover varies.

An offshoot of the New York original, the Mirage's glitzy hip-hop nightclub – the name stands for "One Of A Kind" – is renowned for high-profile guest appearances,

Señor Frog's

including a New Year's Eve DJ set by Kanye West. Decorated with zebra-stripe flooring and a dozen artworks by Roy Nachum, it's capable of holding well over a thousand people. Each of its two separate rooms has its own DJ booth, but most of the tables are reserved for patrons prepared to pay high prices for bottle service.

Encore Beach Club

MAP P.64, POCKET MAP J1
Encore, 3121 Las Vegas Blvd S ☎ 702 770 7300, ⓦ encorebeachclub.com. Sat 10am–7pm, Fri & Sun 11am–7pm. Cover $20–60.

This luxurious multilevel complex of pools, patios, bars and private bungalows, in front of Encore but still thoroughly screened from the Strip, has to be the definitive expression of Las Vegas's recent craze for DJ-fuelled daytime poolside parties. No money could buy the worldwide publicity it received as the scene of Prince Harry Windsor's notorious antics in 2012, so not surprisingly it's now even more packed than ever. Exhausted revellers can escape the crowds either on pristine white "lily pads" out

in the water or in private cabanas, but the pounding music will follow you everywhere. Expect to pay ultra-high prices even for regular bar drinks, let alone table service.

Tao

MAP P.64, POCKET MAP J5
Second Level, Venetian, 3355 Las Vegas Blvd S ☎ 702 388 8338, ⓦ venetian.com. Nightclub Thurs–Sat 10.30pm–5am; Tao Beach late April–Oct daily 10am–sunset. Cover Thurs & Fri $20, Sat $40; weekend wristband $100 (cover and fees subject to change).

An immediate hit in 2005 and still very much the place to be seen, this dynamic high-concept Asian-style nightclub inevitably attracts larger crowds than its small dance floor can handle. Even on the guest list you'll have to wait to get in and you'll pay heavily for any private space. The open-air *Tao Beach* pool club is a great place to gear up for the evening. Weekend wristbands also give admission to the same owners' *Lavo* club in the adjacent Palazzo.

XS

MAP P.64, POCKET MAP J1
Encore, 3121 Las Vegas Blvd S ☎ 702 521

4005, Ⓦ xslasvegas.com. Fri–Sun from 10.30pm. Cover $20–30, but subject to change.

Where do *Encore's* beautiful people go when they've had enough pool time at the beach club? To the even more decadent *XS* nightclub, of course. Stay in the tropical mood by throwing some moves on the massive dancefloor and drinking very classy cocktails.

Shows

Human Nature Jukebox

MAP P.64, POCKET MAP H4
Venetian, 3355 Las Vegas Blvd S ☎ 702 414 9000, Ⓦ humannaturelive.com. Tues–Sat 7.30pm. $67–127.

Having enjoyed huge success with their own material back home, wholesome Australian vocal quartet Human Nature moved to Las Vegas, where their show proved enough of a smash to transfer from the (now defunct) Imperial Palace to the Venetian in 2013. Their unlikely Stateside mission, to add a Down-Under twist to the Motown sound, enjoys the personal blessing of Smokey Robinson himself. And no wonder – with their fabulous voices and very likeable energy, they really are superb. A smokin' live band plays the music, and the boys simply soar.

Le Rêve

MAP P.64, POCKET MAP J2
Wynn Las Vegas, 3131 Las Vegas Blvd S ☎ 702 770 9966, Ⓦ wynnlasvegas.com. Mon, Tues & Fri–Sun 7pm & 9.30pm. $115–175.

Le Rêve – "The Dream" – is also the title of Steve Wynn's favourite personal Picasso and was the working name of his casino too. For the show itself, Wynn dreamed of hiring former Cirque du Soleil talent to out-Cirque Cirque with an even more unbelievable extravaganza of colour and spectacle, featuring more water than *O* and wilder costumes than

Mystère. In terms of sheer looks it succeeds, with astonishing *coups de théâtre*; you'll need to overlook the vacuity of the plot, though, in which the endlessly bemused protagonist dreams of finding "the answer to life".

Love

MAP P.64, POCKET MAP F5
Mirage, 3400 Las Vegas Blvd S ☎ 702 792 7777, Ⓦ cirquedusoleil.com. Tues–Sat 7pm & 9.30pm. $86–196.

A genuinely triumphant collaboration of Cirque du Soleil and The Beatles, in which Cirque perform superbly choreographed dancing and acrobatics to a crystal-sharp Beatles soundtrack, *Love* is much, much more than just another "jukebox musical". There's no story and no attempt to depict The Beatles as actual people – though eerily we hear their voices in retrieved studio chatter – just a dazzling celebration of their music and the times and places that made them who they were.

Mystère

MAP P.64, POCKET MAP G3
TI, 3300 Las Vegas Blvd S ☎ 702 894 7722, Ⓦ cirquedusoleil.com. Sat–Wed 7pm & 9.30pm. $69–125.

Twenty-five years since it first opened at Treasure Island, Las Vegas's original Cirque du Soleil show is still arguably the best – you can see why it changed the Strip's entertainment scene forever, overnight. *Mystère* is pure spectacle, from its gorgeous costumes and billows of cascading silk to jaw-dropping circus skills and phenomenal feats of strength.

Terry Fator

MAP P.64, POCKET MAP F4
Mirage, 3400 Las Vegas Blvd S ☎ 702 792 7777, Ⓦ mirage.com. Mon–Thurs 7.30pm. $61–164.

Yes, this middle-American ventriloquist swaps corny jokes with soft-toy puppets, but he also has an extraordinary talent: an astonishing five-octave singing voice that delivers perfect impressions of artists from Ozzy Osbourne to Etta James – all without moving his lips. Despite rocketing to fame and fortune since he won *America's Got Talent* in 2007, he is still likeable and down-to-earth.

Wedding chapels

Chapel of the Bells

MAP P.64, POCKET MAP L3
2233 Las Vegas Blvd S ☎ 702 735 6803, ⓦ chapelofthebellslasvegas.com. Mon–Thurs & Sun 9am–9pm, Fri & Sat 9am–midnight.

Crammed up against the singularly unprepossessing *Fun City Motel*, just north of Sahara Avenue, this little chapel conceals a romantic heart beneath its garish exterior. Draped in white silk, with the sun streaming in, it's really quite attractive – and if it was good enough for Pele, it's good enough for you. Non-denominational weddings start at $175; pay $255 or more and you get free transport to and from your hotel plus a DVD of the service.

Chapel of the Flowers

MAP P.64, POCKET MAP M1

1717 Las Vegas Blvd S ☎ 702 735 4331, ⓦ littlechapel.com. Mon–Sat 7am–9pm, Sun 9am–8pm.

With three separate chapels opening onto the same garden and couples queuing to take snaps at the waterfall, things can get a bit hectic at peak times, but in principle it's all surprisingly tasteful. Most popular is the Victorian chapel, with its marble floors and mahogany pews. Packages, categorized as Intimate, Elegant or Legendary, range from $299 to $9100.

A Little White Wedding Chapel

MAP P.64, POCKET MAP F14
1301 Las Vegas Blvd S ☎ 702 382 5943, ⓦ alittlewhitechapel.com. Daily 8am–midnight.

The definitive only-in-Vegas wedding chapel, as used by Joan Collins and Michael Jordan, not to mention Britney, has grown and grown to include five separate chapels. Four resemble reasonably pleasant areas in, say, a chain hotel; the fifth, the notorious "Tunnel of Love", is basically the former driveway, roofed over with angels painted on the ceiling, and hosts drive-through weddings from as little as $75 (bring your own car).

A Little White Wedding Chapel

Downtown Las Vegas

Amounting, as far as visitors are concerned, to little more than three or four blocks, downtown is where Las Vegas started out when the railroad arrived in 1905, and also held its first casinos back in the 1930s. Many visitors prefer downtown to the Strip, feeling that by offering serious gambling, plus cheap bars, restaurants and buffets, its no-nonsense casinos represent the "real" Las Vegas. With its old-style neon signs and garish arrays of multicoloured light bulbs, it also looks much more like the Las Vegas of popular imagination than the high-tech Strip, while in the artificial sky of the Fremont Street Experience canopy it boasts a genuine must-see attraction. What's more, thanks to revitalization efforts that include the opening of the intriguing Mob Museum and the highbrow Smith Center arts centre, downtown finally appears to be on the way back up again.

Fremont Street Experience

MAP P.80, POCKET MAP G12
Fremont St, between Main and Fourth sts ☎ 702 678 5600, Ⓦ vegasexperience. com. Nightly, on the hour from sunset until 1am. Free.

Wanting to give downtown a large-scale spectacle to match the Strip and make visitors feel safer outdoors at night, the downtown casinos came up with an amazing rebranding scheme – they put a roof over four city blocks and renamed downtown the **Fremont Street Experience**. After dark, the sky itself seems to become a giant movie screen – a dazzling light show of monsters and mayhem. Live bands pump out rock classics on stages set up at the main intersections – and downtown parties until long after midnight.

SlotZilla

MAP P.80, POCKET MAP G12
Fremont St ☎ 844 947 8342, Ⓦ vegasexperience.com. Mon–Thurs & Sun 1pm–1am; Fri & Sat 1pm–2am. Zipline $25, Zoomline $45. Weight restrictions apply.

Unveiled in 2013, **SlotZilla** is an extraordinary two-tier zip line centring on the world's biggest slot machine. The 120ft-tall monstrosity ejects four riders at a time on each level. The lower Zipline has seats; riders on the upper Zoomline fly like Superman through the canopy of the Fremont Street Experience.

The Plaza

MAP P.80, POCKET MAP F11
1 Main St ☎ 702 386 2110, Ⓦ plazahotelcasino.com.

Once Las Vegas's railroad station, the huge **Plaza** casino looked set to shut up shop in 2010. Surprisingly, it reopened within a year following a $35 million face-lift. Its owners cannily bought up the furnishings of the abandoned Fontainebleu, and the re-vamped Plaza now holds some of downtown's best bars and restaurants, including Oscar Goodman's glass-domed steakhouse (see page 84).

The Golden Gate

MAP P.80, POCKET MAP G11

1 E Fremont St ☎ 702 385 1906,
ⓦ goldengatecasino.com.
Having opened in 1906, the
Golden Gate is only a year younger
than the city itself. A railroad hotel
before becoming a casino, it still
has only a hundred rooms and
remains an appealing historical
anomaly. Recent modernizations
have stripped away some of its
charms, unfortunately.

Golden Nugget

MAP P.80, POCKET MAP G12
129 E Fremont St ☎ 702 385 7111,
ⓦ goldennugget.com/lasvegas.
Downtown's largest and highest-
profile casino, the **Golden Nugget**
has more in common with the
Strip than with its neighbours.
Built in 1946, it's among the city's
oldest casinos, but its current
incarnation owes more to the
1970s, when it was acquired by a
young man who was to become
the leading entrepreneur of
modern Las Vegas: Steve Wynn.
Downtown has traditionally been
characterized by "sawdust joints";
Wynn gave the Golden Nugget
the bright, glittery feel it retains
to this day.

The most visible result of
remodelling by its latest owners is
the open-air swimming pool at its
heart; guests who plummet down its
towering waterslide pass in a clear
tube through a shark-filled aquarium.

Most recently, the casino opened
up its Fremont Street facade, adding
Bar 46 to create a prime vantage
point for the light show on Fremont
Street. The casino holds little for
sightseers other than an actual
golden nugget; the 62-pound,
million-dollar Hand of Faith was
found in Australia in 1980.

Binion's Gambling Hall

MAP P.80, POCKET MAP G12
128 E Fremont St ☎ 702 382 1600,
ⓦ binions.com.
If you think owning a casino is
a sure-fire way to make money,
Binion's Gambling Hall offers
a salutary lesson. When its
original owner, Benny Binion,
died in 1989, this was, as Binion's
Horseshoe, Las Vegas's most
profitable casino. His heirs ran
the place so badly that it lost its
rooms and even its name. Caesars
Entertainment briefly bought it to
acquire the Horseshoe name and

Golden Nugget

the World Series of Poker, but sold it on.

Binion's today is in a sorry state, with big empty spaces devoid even of slot machines. Its one gimmick is that visitors can pose for free photos with a million dollars in cash; it takes half an hour to get your print.

Four Queens

MAP P.80, POCKET MAP G12
202 E Fremont St ☏ 702 385 4011,
Ⓦ fourqueens.com.

Opened in 1966 and named for its owner's four daughters, the **Four Queens** fills a whole block of Fremont Street. Its basic role is to soak up any spillover from the Golden Nugget; it holds little apart from a decent pub, the *Chicago Brewing Company* and the *Canyon Club* showroom/nightclub.

Fremont Hotel

MAP P.80, POCKET MAP G12

200 E Fremont St ☏ 702 385 3232,
Ⓦ fremontcasino.com.

Ranking a distant second behind the Golden Nugget in terms of glitz and glamour, but still ahead of its other downtown neighbours, the **Fremont Hotel** is a smart but otherwise unremarkable casino. Back in 1956 this was Nevada's tallest building; now it's noteworthy as the home of above-par restaurants, and little else.

The D

MAP P.80, POCKET MAP G12
301 E Fremont St ☏ 800 274 5825, Ⓦ thed.com.

A rare example of a casino completely changing both its image and its name, **The D** was until a few years ago a fake-Irish joint called Fitzgeralds, guarded by Mr O'Lucky the leprechaun. The "D" stands for downtown and Detroit, hometown of owner, Derek Stevens. He's taken advantage of

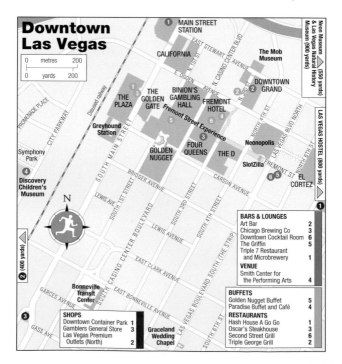

Downtown Las Vegas

| 0 | metres | 200 |
| 0 | yards | 200 |

MAIN STREET STATION

CALIFORNIA

The Mob Museum

Neon Museum & Las Vegas Natural History Museum (900 yards)

(550 yards)

THE PLAZA
THE GOLDEN GATE
BINION'S GAMBLING HALL
FREMONT HOTEL
DOWNTOWN GRAND

Greyhound Station

Fremont Street Experience

GOLDEN NUGGET
FOUR QUEENS
THE D

Neonopolis

LAS VEGAS HOSTEL (800 yards)

Symphony Park

Discovery Children's Museum

SlotZilla
EL CORTEZ

Bonneville Transit Center

Graceland Wedding Chapel

BARS & LOUNGES
Art Bar 2
Chicago Brewing Co 3
Downtown Cocktail Room 6
The Griffin 5
Triple 7 Restaurant and Microbrewery 1
VENUE
Smith Center for the Performing Arts 4

BUFFETS
Golden Nugget Buffet 5
Paradise Buffet and Café 4
RESTAURANTS
Hash House A Go Go 1
Oscar's Steakhouse 3
Second Street Grill 6
Triple George Grill 2

SHOPS
Downtown Container Park 1
Gamblers General Store 3
Las Vegas Premium Outlets (North) 2

the most unusual feature, that the casino has two storeys, to give each a different character – a contemporary style at street level, where go-go dancers gyrate in the "party pit", and vintage upstairs. Entertainment includes live music and comedy, plus a murder-mystery dinner theatre.

El Cortez

MAP P.80, POCKET MAP H12
600 E Fremont St ☏ 702 385 5200,
🌐 elcortezhotelcasino.com.

Long celebrated as downtown's most cheerfully downmarket casino, the seventy-year-old **El Cortez** is looking remarkably spruce thanks to a freshly remodelled facade. For a taste of days gone by, as well as cheap dining and some of the best gambling odds around, it's worth braving the slightly intimidating five-minute walk east of the Fremont Street Experience even if you're not staying here.

Main Street Station

MAP P.80, POCKET MAP G11
200 N Main St ☏ 702 387 1896,
🌐 mainstreetcasino.com.

At a little over twenty years old, **Main Street Station**, just north of the Plaza, is downtown's youngest major casino. Despite its antique-filled Victoriana theme, it's also among the brightest casinos. While it doesn't belong to the Station chain ubiquitous elsewhere in the city, it offers a similar range of restaurants and bars.

The Neon Museum

MAP P.80, POCKET MAP H10
770 Las Vegas Blvd N ☏ 702 387 6366,
🌐 neonmuseum.org. Tours daily from 9am onwards, precise schedules vary. Day tours $19, after-dark tours $25.

If your appetite is whetted by the vintage signs displayed along Fremont Street, east of Las Vegas Boulevard, take a tour of the **Neon Museum** half a mile north. Treasuring signs and sculptures

El Cortez

salvaged from long-lost casinos like the Desert Inn and the Hacienda, this is basically a junkyard, without even restrooms. Come after dark to see it at its best. The visitor centre was once the space-age lobby of *La Concha Motel*.

The Mob Museum

MAP P.80, POCKET MAP G11
300 Stewart Ave ☏ 702 229 2734,
🌐 themobmuseum.org. Sun–Wed 9am–10pm, Thurs–Sat 9–12am; $27, ages 11–17 $17, under-11s free.

Opened on February 14, 2012, the 83rd anniversary of the Saint Valentine's Day Massacre, Las Vegas's **Mob Museum** was designed as the lynchpin of a campaign by then-mayor Oscar Goodman – a former lawyer who defended many underworld figures – to revitalize downtown as a tourist destination. Its full name, the National Museum of Organized Crime and Law Enforcement, reflects its dual goal of chronicling the mobsters who once controlled the city and the lawmen who eventually brought them down.

The museum takes up three storeys of the imposing former federal courthouse, two blocks north of Fremont Street. One upstairs courtroom has been restored to how it looked in 1950 when it hosted hearings by Senator Estes' Senate committee investigating organized crime.

With its comprehensive displays giving the inside stories on all sorts of Las Vegas characters and conspiracies, the Mob Museum is a fascinating place to spend a few hours. It likes to pitch itself as offering a serious perspective on the city's entanglement with the underworld; however, it has a disconcerting propensity for trivializing or glamorizing Las Vegas's gangster past. Lurid panels detail, for example, the "Mob's Greatest Hits", while waxworks depict gory corpses.

Discovery Children's Museum

MAP P.80, POCKET MAP F12
360 Promenade Place ☎ 702 382 3445, ⓦ discoverykidslv.org. June–Sept Mon–Sat 10am–5pm, Sun noon–5pm; Oct–May Tues–Fri 9am–4pm, Sat 10am–5pm, Sun noon–5pm; ages 1–99 $14.50.

Safely ensconced in spacious new premises, next to the Smith Center half a mile west of Fremont Street, the long-established **Discovery Children's Museum** remains a favourite with younger children in particular. Centring on the three-storey indoor Summit Tower, with twelve levels of interactive science exhibits, it also holds play areas such as a medieval castle.

Las Vegas Natural History Museum

MAP P.80, POCKET MAP H10
900 Las Vegas Blvd N ☎ 702 384 3466, ⓦ lvnhm.org. Daily 9am–4pm. $12, ages 3–11 $6.

Collections at the **Las Vegas Natural History Museum**, a mile north of downtown, range from stuffed lions to animatronic dinosaurs, complemented by tanks of live sharks and snakes. One remarkable specimen, a dinosaur that was naturally mummified before it became a fossil, prompts an intriguing CSI-style investigation into its life and death. There's also a replica of Tutankhamun's tomb, donated by the Luxor when it stripped away its former Egyptian theme.

Las Vegas Natural History Museum

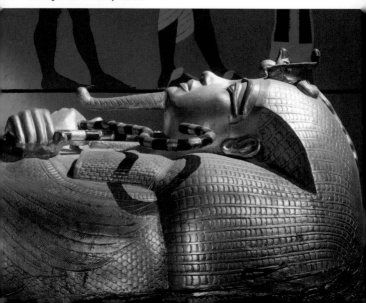

Shops

Downtown Container Park

707 Fremont St ⓦ downtowncontainerpark.
com. Retail daily 11am–9pm, restaurants
Mon–Thurs 11am–11pm, Fri–Sat 11–1am,
Sun 10am–11pm.

Located in the heart of downtown
Las Vegas this open-air shopping
centre with unique restaurants
and live entertainment. There is
something for everyone.

Gamblers General Store

MAP P.80, POCKET MAP F13
800 S Main St ☎ 702 382 9903,
ⓦ gamblersgeneralstore.com. Mon–Sat
9am–6pm, Sun 9am–5pm.

If you love gambling, but
sometimes wish you got something
back for your money, this is
the place to come. You can buy
anything from a $1.99 pack
of playing cards used at your
favourite casino to a $3600 roulette
wheel, strategy books and non-
gaming souvenirs.

Las Vegas Premium Outlets (North)

MAP P.80, POCKET MAP E13
875 S Grand Central Parkway ☎ 702 474
7500, ⓦ premiumoutlets.com. Mon–Sat
10am–9pm, Sun 9am–8pm.

A mile west of downtown and
served by SDX buses (see page
117) from the Strip, this huge
mall consists of over 150 stores
accessed via outdoor walkways.
Unlike the south-Strip branch (see
page 32), most are genuinely
"outlets" of well-known brands –
Diesel, Tommy Hilfiger, Nike – so
you can find real bargains.

Buffets

Golden Nugget Buffet

MAP P.80, POCKET MAP G12
Golden Nugget, 129 E Fremont St ☎ 702
386 8152, ⓦ goldennugget.com/lasvegas.
Breakfast Mon–Fri 7–10.30am, $16;
champagne brunch Sat & Sun 7am–3.30pm

Gamblers General Store

$23; lunch Mon–Fri 10.30am–3.30pm $17;
dinner daily 3.30–10pm, Mon–Wed $25,
Thurs & Sat $36, Fri $30, Sun $30.

As you might expect of a casino
once owned by Steve Wynn, the
Golden Nugget boasts downtown's
best buffet, offering various cuisines
in a humdrum space. The weekend
"seafood and more" dinners are the
best bargain.

Paradise Buffet & Café

MAP P.80, POCKET MAP G12
Fremont Hotel, 200 Fremont St ☎ 702 385
3232, ⓦ fremontcasino.com. Breakfast
Mon–Fri 7–10.30am, $9; champagne
brunch Sat & Sun 7am–3pm, $14; lunch
Mon–Fri 11am–3pm, $10, dinner Prime
Rib Night (Sun, Mon & Thurs) $16, Seafood
Fantasy (Tues & Fri) $28, Steak Night (Wed
& Sat) $16.

Downtown has always been
popular with Hawaiian visitors, and
with palm trees and bright colours,
the Fremont's buffet gives a taste
of the islands themselves. The food
concentrates on American classics;
prices go up for the "Seafood
Fantasy" (Tues and Fri). There is
also a separate café menu.

Restaurants

Hash House A Go Go

MAP P.80, POCKET MAP F11

The Plaza, 1 Main St ☎ 702 386 4646, Ⓦ hashhouseagogo.com/vegas. Mon–Thurs & Sun 7.30am–10pm, Fri & Sat 7am–10pm. This gleaming, all-day diner is hardly the place for a romantic rendezvous, but its "twisted farm food" – obscenely large portions of wholesome American country classics like pot pie – tastes good and is great value. It's best for breakfast, with a varied menu.

Oscar's Steakhouse

MAP P.80, POCKET MAP F11
The Plaza, 1 Main St ☎ 702 386 7227, Ⓦ oscarslv.com. Daily 5–10pm.
Perched in a glass bubble overlooking Fremont Street, this shameless bid by former mayor Oscar Goodman to cash in on his larger-than-life image is a favourite with all who fondly remember the old Las Vegas. A New York-style steakhouse, serving quality filet mignon or bone-in steaks ($55-plus), it also has an Italian-heavy menu. The hostesses can be hired as dinner companions.

Second Street Grill

MAP P.80, POCKET MAP G12
Fremont Hotel, 200 E Fremont St ☎ 702 385 3232, Ⓦ fremontcasino.com. Wed, Thurs & Sun 5–10pm, Fri & Sat 5–11pm.

Oscar's Steakhouse

Despite its dreary, windowless setting, this gourmet restaurant offers downtown's most inventive cuisine. Asian-influenced fish dishes like the tuna sashimi starter or sesame-crusted *mahi-mahi* reflect its Hawaiian roots, while dishes like chicken breast with risotto and pesto are also on offer. Mains cost $28-plus, while the nightly special rib-eye steak is $37.

Triple George Grill

MAP P.80, POCKET MAP G11
201 N Third St ☎ 702 384 2761, Ⓦ triplegeorgegrill.com. Lunch Mon–Fri 11am–4pm; dinner Fri–Sat 4pm–midnight, Sun–Thurs 4–11pm.
Its speakeasy decor, mixing brickwork with wood panelling, might not be genuine, but this downtown steakhouse is a real hangout for local politicos and lawyers. Come early for lunch and watch them wheeling and dealing in the back room over $9 Caesar salads, $22 airline chicken or steaks costing from $27.

Bars and lounges

Art Bar

MAP P.80, POCKET MAP G11
206 N Third St ☎ 702 719 5100, Ⓦ downtowngrand.com. Fri & Sat 3pm–11pm.
Just off the lobby of the Downtown Grand – formerly the Lady Luck – the *Art Bar* lives up to its name by festooning its ceiling with artworks. It is the ideal place to relax over a cocktail in its plush armchairs, perhaps after visiting the Mob Museum opposite.

Chicago Brewing Co

MAP P.80, POCKET MAP G12
Four Queens, 202 E Fremont St ☎ 702 924 5222, Ⓦ fourqueens.com. Mon–Fri 11.30am–1.30am, Sat & Sun 10am–1.30am.
Fremont Street's best bar and the pick of Las Vegas's few microbreweries is a noisy and

upbeat spot to enjoy American, German and English-style beers, brewed on site and sold individually or in 64-oz, $15 "Growlers". They also serve pizzas, wings and sandwiches.

Downtown Cocktail Room

MAP P.80, POCKET MAP G12
111 Las Vegas Blvd S ☎ 702 880 3696, Ⓦ thedowntowncocktailroom.com. Mon–Sat 4pm–2am.

Aimed at in-the-know locals rather than tourists, this small, dimly lit cocktail lounge, tucked away behind an industrial facade, evokes downtown's long-lost glory days. Expert mixologists create classic and original cocktails ($10–14), plus there's an early evening bar menu and live DJs after 9pm (Tues–Sat).

The Griffin

MAP P.80, POCKET MAP G12
511 Fremont St ☎ 702 382 0577. Mon–Sat 5pm–3am, Sun 9pm–3am.

This cavernous downtown bar is just a short walk from the main cluster of casinos, beyond the Fremont Street Experience, but it's a world away from the downtown norm. In-the-know locals, including a strong hipster contingent, weave through the black velvet curtain guarding the entrance to settle down by the fireside or find a private booth. Everything turns a bit more hectic at weekends, when local bands or DJs strut their stuff in the back room.

Triple 7 Restaurant and Microbrewery

MAP P.80, POCKET MAP G11
Main Street Station, 200 N Main St ☎ 702 386 4442, Ⓦ mainstreetcasino.com. Daily 11am–7am.

This cavernous pub and restaurant, at the heart of the antique-filled casino, is always full of lively, cheery drinkers savouring European brews and substantial portions of good pub grub.

Graceland Wedding Chapel

Venue

Smith Center for the Performing Arts

MAP P.80, POCKET MAP F12
361 Symphony Park Ave ☎ 702 749 2000, Ⓦ thesmithcenter.com. See website for programme and prices.

Las Vegas acquired a performing arts centre in 2012 with the opening of this showpiece Art Deco-influenced theatre half a mile west of downtown. Its two-thousand-seat auditorium hosts classical concerts, ballet and touring Broadway shows, while smaller showrooms put on a varied programme of live music and theatre.

Wedding chapel

Graceland Wedding Chapel

MAP P.80, POCKET MAP G13
619 S Las Vegas Blvd ☎ 702 382 0091, Ⓦ gracelandchapel.com. Daily 9am–11pm.

This pretty chapel, just south of downtown, is "the home of the original Elvis wedding". You can't marry Elvis, and he's not a minister, so he can't marry you, but he can renew your vows. In the basic $199 package, the King walks you down the aisle and sings two songs; pay $799 and you get two "duelling Elvises", young and old.

The rest of the city

A glance at any map will tell you that there's a lot more to Las Vegas than simply downtown and the Strip; well over a million people live in the valley as a whole. This is not a city where under-explored neighbourhoods harbour fascinating and little-known attractions, however. It's a vast and overwhelmingly residential sprawl that you'll need a car and plenty of time to explore at all thoroughly. Even then, almost all you'll find will be casinos, malls, bars and restaurants; this chapter highlights the picks of the bunch. In addition to the few that genuinely compete with the best of the Strip – the Hard Rock Hotel, the Palms and the Rio – it focuses on the so-called "locals casinos" throughout the city. While these can't match the wow factor of the Strip giants, they find their own niche by offering good-value food, drink and entertainment.

Dig This!

MAP P.88, POCKET MAP A11
3012 S Rancho Drive ☎ 702 222 4344,
🌐 digthisvegas.com. Daily 8am–5pm;
advance reservations essential. Big Dig
$269, Mega Dig $485.

Las Vegas has always specialized in making adult fantasies come true, but it took a truly inspired entrepreneur to come up with the idea for **Dig This!**. On a patch of desert waste ground, a mile west of the Strip,

Hard Rock Hotel

customers get to operate their very own piece of heavy machinery. On payment of a substantial fee, anyone aged 14 and over can drive either a bulldozer or an excavator for ninety minutes; that's a Big Dig, while a Mega Dig lets you do both. Not only do you not need a driving licence, you don't even need to be old enough to have one.

After a few minutes' training you're allowed to sit alone in your vehicle, linked via headphones to an instructor who has an override switch. In a bulldozer, you pile up a huge mound of sand and then power the dozer over the top; in an excavator, you dig trenches and play "basketball" using your scoop. The point, of course, is that it's all fantastic fun. Whether they do it as a retirement treat or a hen party escapade, everyone who has a go seems to come away exhilarated.

Dig This!

Gold Coast

MAP P.88, POCKET MAP G15
4000 W Flamingo Rd ☎ 702 367 7111,
🌐 goldcoastcasino.com.

One of Las Vegas's first "locals casinos", targeted at city residents themselves, the **Gold Coast** was erected half a mile west of the Strip in 1986. While it swiftly acquired much fancier neighbours, in the shape of the Rio and the Palms, it's hung on to its rather staid Western decor, and remains geared towards a local crowd, especially from the city's Chinatown immediately to the north. As well as some good Asian restaurants, it also holds a seventy-lane bowling alley.

Hard Rock Hotel

MAP P.88, POCKET MAP B16
4455 Paradise Rd ☎ 702 693 5000,
🌐 hardrockhotel.com.

Flagged by two enormous guitars, the **Hard Rock Hotel** clamours for attention a mile east of the Strip. Best seen as a self-sufficient party resort, it fills every weekend with southern Californians who come to soak up the rock'n'roll atmosphere of its clubs, music venues and "daylife"-oriented pool. For sightseers there's little here apart from endless display cabinets of stage clothes and instruments, from Elvis to Bruce and beyond. Spend a night or two, though (ideally to coincide with a big gig), to enjoy its excellent bars and restaurants, and you might just have the time of your life.

M Resort

MAP P.88
12300 Las Vegas Blvd S, Henderson
☎ 702 797 1000, 🌐 themresort.com.

Surveying the city from its hillside perch near the southern end of the Las Vegas Valley, ten miles south of Mandalay Bay, the shiny **M Resort** opened in 2009. Sadly, the economic climate was far from ideal for the smartest new off-Strip casino to be built in many years, so despite its impressive contemporary architecture and well-considered amenities it was soon struggling. Within two years, it was snapped up by Penn Gaming for barely a quarter of its original billion-dollar cost.

Through it all, the M is looking as good as ever – almost in the Wynn class. With lavish public spaces including a lovely Palm Springs-style pool complex and great restaurants like the hugely popular *Studio B* buffet and irresistible *Baby Cakes* bakery, it's unusual in appealing to locals and visitors alike.

National Atomic Testing Museum

MAP P.88, POCKET MAP B12

755 E Flamingo Rd 🕾 702 794 5151, Ⓦ nationalatomictestingmuseum.org. Mon–Sat 10am–5pm, Sun noon–5pm. $22, senior citizens $18, students and ages 7–14 $16, under-6s free.

Between 1951 and 1958, a remote desert area sixty miles northwest of Las Vegas, designated as the Nevada Test Site, was used for above-ground tests of atomic bombs. Mushroom clouds were visible from the city and tourists

would time their holidays so they could watch the blasts. That astonishing saga is explored in the **National Atomic Testing Museum**, which covers not only the political, scientific and military background, but also the kitschy ways in which popular culture celebrated the bomb. A separate **Area 51** exhibit examines the even more unbelievable story of supposed "alien autopsies" in the same general vicinity.

Orleans

MAP P.88, POCKET MAP A12

4500 W Tropicana Ave 🕾 702 365 7111, Ⓦ orleanscasino.com.

Owned by the same management as the Gold Coast (see page 87), to which it's linked by free shuttles, the **Orleans** is roughly a mile due west of New York–New York. Several of its restaurants and bars play on the New Orleans connection suggested by its name, but really the emphasis is on

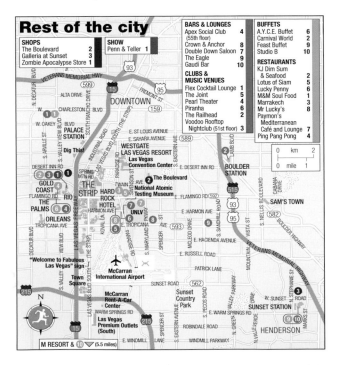

catering to more local tastes, via such means as an eighteen-screen cinema and 24-hour bowling alley. As a place to gamble at above-average odds and then relax over cheap food and entertainment, it's hard to beat.

The Palms

MAP P.88, POCKET MAP F16
4321 W Flamingo Rd ☎ 702 942 7777,
Ⓦ palms.com.

It's a cruel drawback of running a relatively small off-Strip casino that as soon as you come up with brilliant ideas to lure visitors, the big boys simply copy your innovations and entice your customers back. When it opened across from the Rio in 2001, the **Palms** became the first Las Vegas casino to tap into the twenty-first century's mix of street and celebrity culture, with an array of youth-oriented clubs and theatres that made it the hippest hangout in the city. Since then, the Strip giants have added their own state-of-the-art nightclubs and the Palms has had to keep upping its game.

Despite recent money worries, the basic elements of the Palms' winning formula remain pretty much intact. Nightlife options including the penthouse *Moon* club and the *Apex* still draw in the crowds, while the Pearl Theater ranks among the city's premier concert venues. The Palms even houses a world-class recording studio, used by artists from Lady Gaga and Katy Perry to Usher and Tony Bennett. And with its own cinema, some decent budget restaurants and a good-value buffet, it's careful not to neglect locals either.

Rio

MAP P.88, POCKET MAP H15
3700 W Flamingo Rd ☎ 866 746 7671,
Ⓦ caesars.com/rio-las-vegas.

A proud purple beacon, half a mile west of Caesars Palace across the interstate, when it opened in 1990, the **Rio** looked as though it might become the first casino in a

National Atomic Testing Museum

generation to threaten the Strip's domination. It was independently owned and played on its Rio de Janeiro theme to build a reputation as the city's premier party scene for locals and visitors alike. Then, as now, all its guest rooms were sizeable suites, sold at highly competitive rates.

In 1999, however, the Rio was sold for almost a billion dollars to what later became Caesars Entertainment. Now run as an adjunct to its sister properties on the central Strip – to which it's linked by free shuttle buses (daily 10am–1am) from Harrah's (see page 55) and Bally's (see page 51) – it can therefore seem like something of an afterthought.

Every June and July, the Rio hosts the high-profile **World Series of Poker**; Caesars acquired the rights to the tournament when it purchased its previous home, Binion's Horseshoe, in 2004. For the rest of the year, it's best known for its sky-high *VooDoo Rooftop Nightclub* (see page 95), the Penn and Teller magic show (see page 95) and its fine selection of restaurants and buffets.

The Rio is also home to the **VooDoo Zipline** ($27.50; daily 11am–11pm), a thrill ride that connects the rooftops of its two towers, nearly 500ft above ground level. Participants

Rio

are strapped into exposed side-by-side seats, and the experience resembles riding in the scariest ski lift you ever saw.

Sam's Town

MAP P.88, POCKET MAP D12
5111 Boulder Hwy ☎ 702 456 7777,
🌐 samstownlv.com.

Best known these days as the name of an album by Las Vegas's favourite home-grown band, The Killers, **Sam's Town** is a locals casino that stands six miles east of the Strip, alongside the main road out to the Hoover Dam. While maintaining its long-standing Wild West image, it has flirted in recent years with new affiliations such as NASCAR racing, hosting the now-defunct Sam's Town 300 race. It has also roofed over its central courtyard, adding gardens and waterfalls to create Mystic Falls Park, the scene of regular sound-and-light shows (daily 2pm, 6pm, 8pm & 10pm).

Sunset Station

MAP P.88, POCKET MAP D13
1301 W Sunset Rd, Henderson ☎ 702 547 7777, 🌐 sunsetstation.sclv.com.

The self-styled "Spanish Mediterranean" **Sunset Station** casino was the first major casino to be built in the fast-growing suburb of Henderson, eight miles southeast of the Strip. It opened in 1997 as the flagship property of the so-called "Stations chain" of locals casinos, and while the chain as a whole has experienced financial uncertainties in recent years, Sunset Station itself is still looking good.

Its primary customers being drawn from its own neighbourhood, Sunset Station is crammed with community assets like the huge 72-lane, 24-hour StrikeZone bowling alley, a 13-screen cinema, and, rather more questionably, the Kids Quest daycare centre that'll look after children while their parents are gambling. Some of its features would be impressive even on the Strip, however, including the amazing undulating *Gaudí Bar* (see page 94), which is the centrepiece of the casino floor.

Westgate Las Vegas Resort

MAP P.88, POCKET MAP L5
3000 Paradise Rd ☎ 702 732 5111,
🌐 westgateresorts.com.

The **Westgate Las Vegas Resort** used to be the largest and most famous hotel in the world. Built by legendary entrepreneur Kirk Kerkorian in 1969, half a mile east of the Strip, it was originally the International Hotel. Renamed the Las Vegas Hilton four years later, it earned its place in history by hosting Elvis Presley for 837 sell-out concerts, starting with his comeback appearance in July 1969 and continuing until his final Las Vegas appearance in December 1976. A bronze statue now commemorates the King's achievements. Neither having its own Monorail station nor standing next to the city's Convention Center spared it a battering by the recession, however, and in 2012 it went into foreclosure and lost the Hilton name. Its restaurants and music venues are still just about ticking along, but it feels very peripheral indeed.

Shops

The Boulevard

MAP P.88, POCKET MAP B12

3528 S Maryland Parkway ☎ 702 735 7430, ⓦ boulevardmall.com. Mon–Sat 10am–9pm, Sun 11am–7pm.
A landmark for local shoppers since 1966 – long before anyone dreamed of opening stores on the Strip – the Boulevard mall is still going strong. Anchored by the likes of Macy's and JC Penney, it's a handy stop-off for day-to-day shopping.

Galleria at Sunset

MAP P.88, POCKET MAP D13

1300 W Sunset Rd, Henderson ☎ 702 434 0087, ⓦ galleriaatsunset.com. Mon–Sat 10am–9pm, Sun 11am–6pm.
Massive suburban shopping mall across from Sunset Station, eight miles southeast of the Strip, with five department stores and a host of middle-American chains.

Zombie Apocalypse Store

MAP P.88, POCKET MAP A12

3420 Spring Mountain Rd ☎ 866 784 7882. Daily: summer 10am–9pm, winter 10am–7pm.

Everything you'll need to cope with the impending zombie apocalypse, from emergency rations to knives and swords. You can also sign up to spend an evening shooting "real zombies", with real paintball guns.

Buffets

A.Y.C.E. Buffet

MAP P.88, POCKET MAP F16

The Palms, 4321 W Flamingo Rd ☎ 702 953 7679, ⓦ palms.com. Breakfast Mon–Sat 8–11am $10; brunch Sun 8am–4pm $22; lunch Mon–Sat 11am–4pm $15; dinner daily 4–9pm $22.
A bright, modern space adjoining the main casino floor, the Palms' buffet (A.Y.C.E. stands for All You Can Eat) is popular with locals for its ease of access and range of world cuisines; be sure to sample the succulent ham hock.

Carnival World

MAP P.88, POCKET MAP H15

Rio, 3700 W Flamingo Rd ☎ 702 777 7777, ⓦ caesars.com/rio-las-vegas. Champagne brunch Sat & Sun 10am–3pm $27; dinner weekdays 4–9pm $32, or $35 weekend dinner.

The Boulevard

M&M Soul Food

Crowds flock to the Rio's buffet to pile their plates with everything from sushi to corndogs; the choice is endless, even if the quality is only exceptional in the evening's sumptuous seafood spread.

Feast Buffet

MAP P.88, POCKET MAP D13
Sunset Station, 1301 W Sunset Rd
☎ 702 547 7777, ⓦ sunsetstation.sclv.
com. Breakfast Mon–Sat 8–11am $10;
brunch Sun 8am–4pm $16; lunch Mon–Sat
11am–4pm $13; dinner daily 4–9pm $116.
Unlike their Strip rivals, all the Stations casinos still offer cut-price buffets to lure Las Vegans out to eat and gamble. Sunset Station has the nicest dining room; pick carefully and you can get a great-value meal including dishes like Indian curries, seldom seen elsewhere.

Studio B

MAP P.88
M Resort, 12300 Las Vegas Blvd S ☎ 877
673 7678, ⓦ themresort.com. Lunch
Mon–Thurs 11am–2.30pm $17; brunch Fri
11am–2pm $25, Sat & Sun 11am–8.30pm

$42; dinner Mon–Thurs 2.30–8.30pm $25,
Fri 2.30–8.30pm $42.
Primarily this is a buffet, with food (and prices) to match the very best on the Strip, but it's also a "studio" because chefs demonstrate their art here on stage and TV screens. Prices include free wine and beer; the higher evening and weekend rates cover seafood spreads that include raw oysters. Allow time to get here – it's ten miles south of the Strip – and expect to queue to get in.

Restaurants

KJ Dim Sum & Seafood

MAP P.88, POCKET MAP H15
Rio, 3700 W Flamingo Rd ☎ 702 777
7777, ⓦ caesars.com/rio-las-vegas. Daily
10am–2am.
This offshoot of a popular restaurant in Las Vegas's nearby Chinatown has been an instant hit, especially for lunching locals who come to select $3–6 dumplings and seafood specialities from the gleaming dim sum trolleys. Later on, full-sized mains like sizzling

scallops or whole steamed fish cost $20–30.

Lotus of Siam

MAP P.88, POCKET MAP B12
620 E Flamingo Rd ☎ 702 735 3033,
Ⓦ lotusofsiamlv.com. Lunch Mon–Fri
11am–2.30pm; dinner Mon–Sun
5.30–10pm.

Lotus's reputation has followed it to its temporary home on Restaurant Row. The Northern Thai menu is famous for its garlic prawns ($27) and duck dishes, such as *khao soi* ($26), strips of roast duck and crispy skin in a mild curry sauce.

Lucky Penny

MAP P.88, POCKET MAP F16
Palms, 4321 W Flamingo Rd ☎ 702 953
7682, Ⓦ palms.com. Daily 24hr.

Refuel on comfort food, day or night. The mid-century modern-inspired café provides plush seating and spacious booths. At breakfast try the $14 Penny Bennies (ham and eggs on garlic toast with hollandaise), and for a late-night snack, dip waffle-grilled cheese into a cup of tomato soup ($13). Shakes are served boozy or virgin.

M&M Soul Food

MAP P.88, POCKET MAP A11
3923 W Charleston Blvd ☎ 702 453 7685.
Daily 7am–8pm.

Genuine soul food being hard to come by in Las Vegas, this neighbourhood diner is a godsend. Four miles west of downtown, it's best reached by car; you won't be in a fit state to walk anywhere once you've filled up on a $15 plate of their tasty chicken, ribs, gumbo or cornbread.

Marrakech

MAP P.88, POCKET MAP B12
3900 Paradise Rd ☎ 702 737 5611,
Ⓦ marrakechvegas.com. Daily 5.30–11pm.

All-you-can-eat banquets of rich, tasty Moroccan food, costing $50 per person and eaten with your fingers from low-lying tables where you sit on scattered cushions. Meaty couscous and pastry dishes are complemented by seafood alternatives, and followed by heavy desserts. Come to enjoy the Middle Eastern atmosphere, belly dancers and all; this is not a place for a quick meal on your own.

Mr Lucky's

MAP P.88, POCKET MAP A16
Hard Rock Hotel, 4455 Paradise Rd ☎ 702
693 5592, Ⓦ hardrockhotel.com. Daily 24hr.

A refreshing modern take on the traditional Las Vegas all-night casino coffee shop, with an open kitchen and stylish patio seating. Whether you grab a prime rib French dip sandwich for lunch ($16) or stumble in for 4am spaghetti and meatballs (also $16), *Mr Lucky's* offers a round-the-clock break from the Hard Rock frenzy.

Paymon's Mediterranean Café and Lounge

MAP P.88, POCKET MAP B12
4147 S Maryland Parkway at Flamingo Rd
☎ 702 731 6030, Ⓦ paymons.com. Daily
11am–12am.

A truly local restaurant, busy until late with students from the nearby university. While not exclusively vegetarian – meat-eaters can enjoy dishes like the $16 broiled chicken kabob – it's especially recommended for its extensive array of Middle Eastern classics such as falafel, hummus and *baba ghanoush*, available singly or in a $15 combination platter.

Ping Pang Pong

MAP P.88, POCKET MAP F15
Gold Coast, 4000 W Flamingo Rd ☎ 702
247 8136, Ⓦ goldcoastcasino.com. Daily
10am–3pm & 5pm–3am.

You can tell straight away that this is the best Chinese restaurant in any Las Vegas casino; most of the diners are Chinese and the menu is written in Chinese characters as well as English. Dim sum makes a lunchtime treat, while later on you can get seafood noodles for just $15 or half a roast duck for $17.

Double Down Saloon

Bars and lounges

Apex Social Club

MAP P.88, POCKET MAP F16
Palms, 4321 W Flamingo Rd ☎ 702 944 5980, ⓦ apexsocialclubcom. Thurs–Sun 8pm–dawn. Cover $25–$35.
From its vantage point of the 55th floor of the Palms, this 8000-sq-ft bar and nightclub offers one of the best panoramas of the city. The sprawling open-air lounge with sofas is designed to facilitate conversations between guests.

Crown & Anchor

MAP P.88, POCKET MAP B12
1350 E Tropicana Ave ☎ 702 739 8676, ⓦ crownandanchorlv.com. Daily 24hr.
The closest Las Vegas comes to having a genuine British pub – complete with Cornish pasties, ploughman's lunches and Sunday roasts – although most of its customers, even when it's showing European soccer (or rather, football) games, are students from the nearby university.

Double Down Saloon

MAP P.88, POCKET MAP C17
4640 Paradise Rd ☎ 702 791 5775, ⓦ doubledownsaloon.com. Daily 24hr.
Archetypal hole-in-the-wall dive bar, situated one block south of the Hard Rock. The interior features funky murals and a hard-edged punk jukebox. There are no-cover live bands most nights, plus slots, blackjack and pool, and signature drinks like "ass juice" and bacon martinis.

The Eagle

MAP P.88, POCKET MAP C12
3430 E Tropicana Ave ☎ 702 458 8662, no website. Daily 24hr.
This veteran of Las Vegas's gay scene, located four miles east of the Strip, has seen its glitzier rivals come and go, but the regulars still flock in for long-standing nights like the Tues & Fri underwear parties.

Gaudí Bar

MAP P.88, POCKET MAP D13
Sunset Station, 1301 W Sunset Rd, Henderson ☎ 702 547 7777, ⓦ sunsetstation.sclv.com. Daily 24hr.
The coolest bar in any Las Vegas casino, created in honour of Catalan architect Antoni Gaudí, this bizarre fungoid excrescence undulates through the heart of Sunset Station, with cracked-up mosaics across its cave-like walls and light courtesy of the colourful stained-glass panels in the ceiling.

Clubs and music venues

Flex Cocktail Lounge

MAP P.88, POCKET MAP A11
4371 W Charleston Blvd ☎ 702 878 3355 ⓦ flexlasvegas.com. Daily 24hr. No cover.
Lively gay bar and club, with pool tables, slots and an emphasis on upbeat action. Free entertainment nightly, including late-night drag shows. Saturday, plus half-price Happy Hours 4–7pm and 4–7am.

The Joint

MAP P.88, POCKET MAP B16
Hard Rock Hotel, 4455 Paradise Rd ☎ 702 693 5222, ⓦ hardrockhotel.com.
See website for schedule and prices.

Totally revamped in 2009, the Hard Rock's theatre attracts four-thousand-strong crowds to see big-name touring acts. In addition, well-known rock groups take up residence for a month or more at a time, with typical ticket prices of around $100.

Pearl Theater

MAP P.88, POCKET MAP F16
Palms, 4321 W Flamingo Rd ☎ 702 944 3200, Ⓦ palms.com. See website for current schedule and prices.
The Palms' state-of-the-art theatre may be smaller than the Hard Rock's Joint, but with its great sound and atmosphere it attracts its fair share of major-league acts across the spectrum, from hip-hop and R&B to reggae and rock.

Piranha

MAP P.88, POCKET MAP B17
4633 Paradise Rd ☎ 702 791 0100, Ⓦ piranhavegas.com. Daily 10pm–5am. Cover varies, typically $20.
The jewel of the so-called "Fruit Loop" and the pulsating heart of Las Vegas's gay nightlife, the spectacular *Piranha* club is approached via either a fiery waterfall or a piranha-filled aquarium. The similarly lavish *8½ Ultra-lounge* alongside makes a perfect spot to kick off the night.

The Railhead

MAP P.88, POCKET MAP C11
Boulder Station, 4111 Boulder Hwy ☎ 702 432 7777, Ⓦ boulderstation.sclv.com. Daily 24hr. Concert tickets typically $15–40.
A run-of-the-mill member of the Stations chain of locals casinos, Boulder Station's one bright spot is this large lounge/theatre, which hosts Latin nights on Fridays and Sundays, but also puts on solid mid-range country, soul and blues acts.

Voodoo Rooftop Nightclub

MAP P.88, POCKET MAP J15
Rio, 3700 W Flamingo Rd ☎ 702 777 7800, Ⓦ caesars.com/rio-las-vegas. Mon–Thurs & Sun 8pm–2am, Fri & Sat 8pm–3am. Cover $20 and up.
Long famed for its incredible 51st-floor views, this New Orleans-tinged rendezvous made its reputation as an ultra-hip drinking spot. Now a fully fledged nightclub, it's smaller than its newer rivals on the Strip, but the location is as good as ever and offers a great night out at more affordable prices.

Show

Penn & Teller

MAP P.88, POCKET MAP H15
Rio, 3700 W Flamingo Rd ☎ 702 777 2782, Ⓦ pennandteller.com. Mon–Wed, Sat & Sun 9pm, $85–173.
Magicians Penn (the talkative one) and Teller (the other one) have been performing at the Rio since 2000 – while still keeping up their TV careers – but the show remains fresh, whether you simply want to swoon at the magic or you love the behind-the-scenes tricks-of-the-trade patter. They're also great with their audiences, posing and signing happily for groups of fans after the show.

Gaudí Bar

The deserts

Las Vegas stands close to some of the most extraordinary landscapes on the planet – the stark, sublime deserts of the American Southwest. It's possible to get a taste of this red-rock wonderland on brief forays from the city, either to Red Rock Canyon, Hoover Dam and Lake Mead, or to the Valley of Fire. To appreciate its full splendour, however, you need to venture further afield. The primary goal for many visitors is the Grand Canyon, though you'd do better to visit the canyon's South Rim, almost three hundred miles east, than Grand Canyon West, which is closer to hand. Utah's Zion Canyon arguably makes an even better destination for an overnight trip from Las Vegas.

Red Rock Canyon

MAP P.98

17 miles west of the Strip ☏ 702 515 5367, ⓦ redrockcanyonlv.org. Visitor centre daily 8am–4.30pm. Scenic Drive daily: March & Oct 6am–7pm, April–Sept 6am–8pm, Nov–Feb 6am–5pm. $15/vehicle, $5 for bikes, motorbikes and pedestrians.

For a quick blast of dramatic Southwestern scenery and searing desert sun, simply drive west on any road from the Strip. Tucked behind the first low scrubby hills, the **Red Rock Canyon National Conservation Area** centres on a desert basin at the foot of towering 3000ft cliffs. Ideally, come in the morning when the glowing red rocks are spotlit by the rising sun, and the day's heat has yet to set in fully. Staff at the visitor centre will introduce you to this unforgiving but beautiful wilderness, as well as point out the hiking trails and climbing routes that set off from the one-way, thirteen-mile **Scenic Drive** just beyond, which is the only way to see the canyon itself.

Hoover Dam

MAP P.98

30 miles southeast of the Strip ☏ 702 494 2517, ⓦ usbr.gov/lc/hooverdam. Parking daily 8am–5pm; $10. Visitor Center daily, 9am–5pm; $10. Powerplant Tour April–Sept 9.25am–4.55pm; Oct–March 9.25am–3.55pm; $15 including Visitor Center, senior citizens & ages 4–16 $12. Dam Tour April–Sept Mon–Thurs 9.30am–4pm, Fri & Sat 9.30am–4.30pm; Oct–March daily 9.30am–3.45pm; all-inclusive fee $30, no reductions, minimum age 8. Unscheduled maintenance issues mean full tours may not always be available but modified tours are usually offered.

The mighty **Hoover Dam** straddles the Colorado River and thus the Nevada–Arizona state line as well. While this graceful 726ft-tall concrete marvel does not, as many visitors imagine, supply a significant proportion of the electricity that keeps Las Vegas running, its construction during the 1930s triggered the growth spurt, and the gambling boom, that created the modern city.

The main highway to Arizona, US-83, crosses the Colorado on a new bridge, slightly downstream from the dam. To see the dam itself, leave the highway via the spur roads at either end. For a quick look you can park briefly on the Arizona side and walk out atop the dam. Otherwise, park in the multistorey garage on the Nevada side, and walk down to the Visitor Center. Displays there explain the story and inner workings of the dam, but paying just a little extra entitles you to join a Powerplant Tour, and ride an elevator down to its base. The hour-long Dam Tour takes you right into its bowels, to explore its dank and mysterious tunnels.

Lake Mead

MAP P.98
30 miles southeast of the Strip ☎ 702 293 8990, ⓦ nps.gov/lake. Visitor Center daily 9am–4.30pm.

Created by the construction of the Hoover Dam, **Lake Mead**, east of Las Vegas, is the largest artificial lake in the USA when full. Its deep blue waters make an extraordinary contrast against the arid sands and red-rock cliffs of the desert, and attract huge numbers of visitors. Only its Nevada shoreline is accessible by road, most easily via Boulder City, a thirty-mile drive from the Strip.

Call in at the **Visitor Center** just off US-93, which has recently been expanded and renovated and holds some fascinating models and exhibits, then follow the **Lakeshore Scenic Drive** down to the lake itself. How close it approaches the shore depends on current water levels, which have remained low since 2002. Both **Lake Mead Marina** (☎ 702 293 3484, ⓦ riverlakes.com) and the neighbouring **Las Vegas Boat Harbor** (☎ 702 293 1191, ⓦ boatinglakemead.com) rent out boats and jet-skis, while the **Desert Princess** paddle steamer offers lake cruises from the latter ($26–61.50; ☎ 866 292 9191, ⓦ lakemeadcruises.com).

Mount Charleston

A real anomaly in the Nevada deserts, and one that tends to be appreciated more by locals than by visitors, the Spring Mountain range soars into the sky forty miles northwest of the Strip. Its highest peak, **Mount Charleston**, stands just under 12,000ft tall, so its forested slopes offer a welcome

Red Rock Canyon

Grand Canyon West

escape from the summer heat of the city. Several appealing hiking trails set off across the surrounding hillsides.

To reach the mountains, head northwest out of Las Vegas on US-95 then turn west onto Hwy-157, which snakes its way into **Kyle Canyon**. Up at the head of the canyon, the **Mary Jane Falls Trail** is a 2.5-mile round-trip trek that climbs via gruelling switchbacks to a pair of waterfalls. Half a mile further on, the three-mile **Cathedral Rock Trail** involves a demanding thousand-foot ascent to a promontory with onward views to Charleston Peak itself.

That's as far as most people go, but with a little more time you can drive north from Kyle Canyon to **Lee Canyon** along Hwy-158 to enjoy far-reaching views over the desert wasteland where Nevada's notorious A-bomb tests took place in the 1950s, and then return to US-95 via Hwy-56.

Valley of Fire State Park
MAP P.98

Just over 50 miles northeast of the Strip ⓣ 702 397 2088, ⓦ valley-of-fire.com. Visitor centre daily 8.30am–4.30pm. $10/vehicle.

The most mind-blowing red-rock scenery you can see on a driving day-trip lies in the Valley of Fire State Park. To get there, follow I-15 for thirty miles towards Utah, then turn right onto Hwy-169. The park begins just after you cross the ridge of **Muddy Mountain** to look out over a magnificent sandscape of incandescent, multicoloured peaks and cliffs stretching all the way to Lake Mead.

A roadside visitor centre explains local history and geology, and displays live rattlesnakes. It marks the start of a five-mile, dead-end road that winds through amazing rock outcrops that can be explored on short hiking trails. The single most extraordinary formation, however, lies a further three miles along Hwy-169, where a natural arch – **Elephant Rock** – looks like a giant elephant poking its trunk into the sands.

Keep driving east, and you can loop back to Las Vegas along the north shore of **Lake Mead** – a total round trip of 130 miles.

Grand Canyon West

MAP P.98
125 miles east of Las Vegas
ⓦ grandcanyonwest.com. If you drive here yourself you'll still have to join a ground tour, costing minimum $50/person, or $72 including the Skywalk.

The spot known as **Grand Canyon West** (or the West Rim) is not actually in Grand Canyon National Park, but on the Hualapai Indian Reservation to the west. Although it can be reached via a 125-mile one-way drive from Las Vegas, road conditions are so poor that almost all visitors fly (see page 101).

At this point, close to the western end of the Grand Canyon shortly before the Colorado River spills into Lake Mead, the chasm has dwindled to around two miles wide and lacks the extraordinary sculpted rock formations you may be expecting. Instead Grand Canyon West consists of a cluster of viewpoints above drops of up to 4000ft, and looking across to similar cliffs on the far side of the river.

The major attraction is the **Skywalk**, a glass-floored, horseshoe-shaped walkway that juts out over the rim of a side canyon at Eagle Point, close to the airstrip where tours begin. The best view of the canyon itself comes from **Guano Point**, a mile or so north. The Hualapai tribe, who have lived here for over a thousand years, offer various other activities, including dance performances and barbecue cookouts.

Grand Canyon South Rim

MAP P.98
270 miles east of Las Vegas ☎ 928 638 7888, ⓦ nps.gov/grca. Entrance fee $35/ vehicle, valid for seven days.

To see the Grand Canyon in all its glory, you have to visit **Grand Canyon National Park**. This is the area familiar from a million movies and photographs, where the canyon is studded with mighty red-rock buttes and pyramids, and measures a mile deep and eleven miles wide.

Tourist facilities, concentrated around several magnificent viewpoints along the canyon's South Rim, can be reached either by road – a total drive from Las Vegas of 270 miles, via the I-40 interstate that crosses northern Arizona fifty miles south of the canyon – or by air, to Tusayan airport, six miles south of the canyon.

While it's possible to visit the **South Rim** on a day-trip (see box opposite), it makes much more sense to drive yourself and stay at least one night. That will give you the chance to spend some time beside the canyon at sunset and dawn, and to sample the evening atmosphere of the splendid old rim-edge *El Tovar* hotel (see page 113).

Zion National Park

MAP P.98
160 miles northeast of Las Vegas ☎ 435

Grand Canyon South Rim

Grand Canyon tours

The Grand Canyon is not as near Las Vegas as you might imagine. **Grand Canyon National Park** is two hundred miles east of Las Vegas, and the **South Rim** (see page 100), which holds the park's main tourist facilities and viewpoints, is a drive of almost three hundred miles each way from the city. To see the canyon on a day-trip involves a long bus ride or an expensive flight. The majority of tours from Las Vegas therefore go to **Grand Canyon West** (see page 99), more like one hundred miles from the city, which while less spectacular is also home to the **Skywalk**, and offers the chance to land by, and even take a rafting trip on, the **Colorado River**.

With most of the operators listed below, you can choose between taking a **tour** to Grand Canyon West or the South Rim, by bus, helicopter or plane. Bus tours to Grand Canyon West typically cost around $100, or $135 including the Skywalk. The entire round-trip takes at least twelve hours, including four hours at Grand Canyon West itself. A **bus tour** to the South Rim takes over sixteen hours, with less time at the canyon itself. Prices can be as low as $80, but expect to pay more like $150 for a deluxe coach.

Flight-seeing tours to Grand Canyon West start at around $180 by plane (without landing) or $250 by helicopter. Expect to pay at least $250 by plane or $300 by helicopter for a tour that includes walking on the Skywalk, and at least $500 for a helicopter tour that lands down by the river as well.

All **flights** to the South Rim are in fixed-wing planes. A flight with a ground tour of canyon viewpoints by bus will cost around $250. Tours that include a separate helicopter flight once you arrive cost at least $400.

Note that many flights depart not from Las Vegas itself, but from **Boulder City**, thirty miles southeast. If you're hoping for an aerial view of Sin City into the bargain, check which airport your operator uses.

Many tourists highly recommend The Grand Canyon Tour Company's services. Their Grand Canyon West Rim & Skywalk tour costs about $235 but special prices are often available.

TOUR OPERATORS

Grand Canyon Airlines ☎ 702 835 8484, ⊛ grandcanyonairlines.com.
Maverick ☎ 702 261 0007, ⊛ maverickhelicopter.com.
Papillon ☎ 702 736 7243, ⊛ papillon.com.
Scenic Airlines ☎ 702 638 3300, ⊛ scenic.com.
Sundance ☎ 702 736 0606, ⊛ sundancehelicopters.com.
Grand Canyon Tour Company ☎ 702 655 6060,
⊛ grandcanyontourcompany.com.

772 3256, ⊛ nps.gov/zion. Entrance fee $35/vehicle, valid for seven days.
Any Las Vegas visitor hoping to see the stupendous desert scenery of the Southwest at its absolute best would do well to consider making a side trip to **Zion National Park**. Located in southwest Utah, a fast, direct drive of 160 miles northeast up I-15 from Las Vegas, it's every bit as impressive as the Grand Canyon, and offers much greater

potential for an active weekend excursion from the city.

Named by nineteenth-century Mormon settlers, and carved by the Virgin River, Zion Canyon stands at the heart of the park. Unlike at the Grand Canyon, which is almost always seen from above, visitors enter by following the river upstream from the south and therefore see it from the verdant valley below. Astonishing sheer red-rock walls soar to either side, many of them topped by crests of paler sandstone that have been given fanciful names like the Court of the Patriarchs and the Great White Throne.

At the northern end of the canyon, visitors can follow the easy, mile-long **Riverside Walk** to the point where the Virgin River enters the valley. In the Zion Narrows beyond, accessible only to hardy hikers happy to wade waist-deep in ice-cold water, the towering canyon walls stand just a few feet apart. Other demanding trails switchback out

of the valley to reach the desert uplands high above, and make wonderful day-hikes; the **West Rim Trail**, for example, climbs to a slender rock spur known as Angel's Landing, with a sheer quarter-of-a-mile drop to either side. Not surprisingly, Zion is also a favourite destination with rock climbers; several local operators offer guides.

Although it's possible to drive through the southern portion of the park, and continue east (towards Bryce Canyon) via an amazing 1930s tunnel, the only vehicles allowed into the narrowest part of the canyon are free shuttle buses, which depart from the visitor centre beside the park entrance.

In the canyon itself, the veteran *Zion Lodge* (see page 113) offers accommodation and dining, and the park runs large but very pleasant campgrounds. Otherwise, almost all facilities are in the gateway town of **Springdale**, in a magnificent setting just south of the park.

Zion National Park

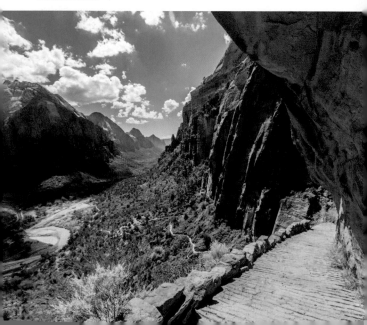

Restaurants

Arizona Room

MAP P.98
Bright Angel Lodge, Grand Canyon South
Rim ☏ 928 638 2631, ⓦ grandcanyonlodges.
com. Daily 11.30am–3pm & 5–9.30pm; Nov
& Dec closed.

This good-value restaurant, near the
rim but with no views, is the most
convenient place to pick up a decent
meal on the South Rim. Lunchtime
burgers, sandwiches and salads cost
$9–13, full dinners more like $18
for chicken and $28 for steak.

Bit & Spur Restaurant

MAP P.98
1212 Zion Park Blvd, Springdale UT ☏ 435
772 3498, ⓦ bitandspur.com. Daily 5–10pm.

With a cosy saloon-like interior,
and a terrace facing Zion's cliffs, this
relaxed but high-quality Mexican/
Southwestern restaurant makes a
wonderful dinner spot. Chilli-
rubbed steak costs $30, barbecued
ribs $28 and a *chile relleno* (stuffed
chilli) just $15, while the outdoor
seating makes an ideal venue for a
beer after a long day's hiking.

Canyon Restaurant & Bar

MAP P.98
The Retreat on Charleston Peak, 2755
Kyle Canyon Rd ☏ 702 872 5500,
ⓦ retreatoncharlestonpeak.com. Breakfast
daily 7am–2pm, bar 11am–close; dinner
Sun–Thurs 5–9pm, Fri & Sat 5–10pm.

With an emphasis on sustainability
and buying local, much of the
produce is sourced from farms
nearby, from the proper coffee
to crispy bacon. The European-
inspired menu includes scallops
and chorizo ($28), pork loin skewer
($23), and a daily special, served at
round tables in a vaulted room.

El Tovar Dining Room

MAP P.98
El Tovar, Grand Canyon South Rim ☏ 928
638 2631, ext 6432, ⓦ grandcanyonlodges.
com. Daily 7–10.30am, 11am–2pm &
5–9pm.

El Tovar Dining Room

The stately splendours of the
timber and stone-built *El Tovar*
make an impressive setting for great
food. Only the front row of tables
enjoy partial views of the canyon,
but this grand century-old hotel
oozes old-fashioned charm and
the waiters are happy to let you
linger. Reserve ahead for dinner,
when mains like half a duck or veal
wienerschnitzel cost around $35;
lunch and breakfast are first-come
first-served and much cheaper.

Mount Charleston Lodge

MAP P.98
5375 Kyle Canyon Rd ☏ 702 872 5408,
ⓦ mtcharlestonlodge.com. Daily 8am–9pm.

The obvious place to stop for lunch
on a Mount Charleston day-trip,
where the road up the mountain
reaches its dead end, featuring
an outdoor patio that enjoys
drop-dead views. The food itself
is less enthralling, with pizzas and
sandwiches for around $15, burgers
a little more and a three-course
dinner menu for $24.

Spotted Dog café

MAP P.98
Flanigan's Inn, 428 Zion Park Blvd,
Springdale UT ☏ 435 772 0700,
ⓦ flanigans.com. Daily 7–11am & 5–10pm.

This very reasonably priced
restaurant is attached to a motel
near the Zion park entrance. In
the morning it lays out a decent
breakfast buffet, while the dinner
menu ranges from a highly
recommended $22 lamb shank to
meatloaf or pasta at more like $15.

ACCOMMODATION

Mandalay Bay Resort

Accommodation

Choosing where to stay is the single biggest decision of any Las Vegas trip. Las Vegas is not like other destinations, where it's the city that you've come to see, and your choice of hotel makes little difference. In Las Vegas, it's the hotels that you've come to see – or rather the stupendously large casino resorts that hold not only the hotels, but also the restaurants, clubs, theatres and attractions, as well as the slot machines and gaming tables. The fundamental choice is whether or not to stay on the Strip, which basically means staying in one of the colossal mega-casinos. Las Vegas is currently home to 32 of the world's 200 largest hotels, most along or very close to the Strip. Between them, they house over 80,000 rooms, an average of almost 4000 each. All of those rooms are at least the standard of a good chain motel, with en-suite bathrooms the norm. Many are much more opulent; the standard rooms at places like Wynn, The Venetian and Bellagio are very plush, while every property offers suites. However, the experience of staying in a hotel that has several thousand rooms has its drawbacks, including long check-in queues (half an hour is considered normal), a lack of personal service and endless walking to and fro. In, say, Caesars Palace or the MGM Grand, it can take twenty minutes to walk from your room out onto the Strip. The result is that most visitors spend their time in either their own hotel or its immediate neighbours. The obvious alternative is to stay downtown, where every hotel is easy walking distance from the rest. But while downtown has more affordable gambling and dining, it has very few shops, shows or clubs, and lacks the jaw-dropping architecture of the Strip. It's possible to find a room elsewhere in the city, in a so-called locals casino, or in one of the many chain motels, but it's not recommended for visitors who want to experience all that makes Las Vegas unique. As for rates, rooms change in price every night according to demand. It's best to book a couple of months or more in advance, or, for weekday stays only, at the very last minute. The prices given here are guidelines to suggest what you might pay during an ordinary, quiet week, and give some idea of how hotels compare.

Resort fees and taxes

Note that in addition to the room rates shown in this chapter, guests in almost every Las Vegas hotel are also required to pay so-called resort fees, listed here separately. These additional daily fees were introduced on the pretext of covering internet access – even if you don't use it – and generally also include such things as local or even long-distance (at Wynn and Encore) phone calls, use of a fitness centre and a newspaper, but *not* parking.

Hotel rates shown here do not include the additional room tax added to all bills, of twelve percent on the Strip, and thirteen percent downtown.

The Strip

ARIA MAP P.40, POCKET MAP B1. 3730 Las Vegas Blvd S ☎ 866 359 7757 or ☎ 702 590 7111, ⓦ aria. com. CityCenter's focal resort, Aria, is perfect for modernists. There's a sleek contemporary aesthetic, and the classy rooms feature big beds, walk-in showers as well as tubs, and on-screen digital controls for everything from curtains to a/c. Check-in can be slow and somewhat anarchic. **Resort fee $39/day. Mon–Thurs & Sun $203, Fri & Sat $300.**

BALLY'S MAP P.50, POCKET MAP G7. 3645 Las Vegas Blvd S ☎ 866 503 4782, ⓦ caesars.com/ballys-las-vegas. Staying at Bally's Is not an experience anyone gets very excited about – the rooms are spacious but otherwise run of the mill – but it is in a great location to make the most of the Strip. Above all, it's connected to its younger sister Paris next door, so guests get the benefits of staying there at much lower rates. **Resort fee $39/ day. Mon–Thurs & Sun from $45, Fri & Sat $270.**

BELLAGIO MAP P.40, POCKET MAP F7. 3600 Las Vegas Blvd S ☎ 888 987 6667 or ☎ 702 693 7111, ⓦ bellagio.com. As Las Vegas is forever outdoing itself, Bellagio is no longer the cream of the crop, but by any normal standards its opulent rooms epitomize luxury, while its location and amenities can't be beaten. The premium rooms overlook the lake and its fountains, but the views from the back, over the pool, are great too. **Resort fee $44/day. Mon–Thurs & Sun $169, Fri & Sat $300.**

CAESARS PALACE MAP P.50, POCKET MAP F6. 3570 Las Vegas Blvd S ☎ 866 227 5938, ⓦ caesars.com/caesars-palace. Fond memories of 1960s excess will always form part of the appeal of Caesars Palace, even if these days comfort tends to win over kitsch. The sheer scale of the place can be overwhelming, but with its top-class dining and shopping, plus a fabulous pool and spa, it still has a real cachet. For serious luxury, pay $50–100 extra to stay in the newer Augustus and Octavius towers, with separate entrances for greater privacy. **Resort fee $40/day. Mon–Thurs & Sun from $109, Fri & Sat from $261.**

CIRCUS CIRCUS MAP P.64, POCKET MAP K8. 2880 Las Vegas Blvd S ☎ 800 634 3450 or ☎ 702 734 0410, ⓦ circuscircus.com. Long a favourite with families and budget travellers, Circus Circus is showing its age; with its neighbours dropping like flies it feels like the casino time forgot. If you don't plan to linger and you have a car, its rock-bottom rates may prove irresistible. Pay a little extra to stay in its renovated towers, as opposed to the dingy Manor section. **Resort fee $30/day. Mon–Thurs & Sun $27, Fri & Sat $120.**

THE COSMOPOLITAN MAP P.40, POCKET MAP F9. 3708 Las Vegas Blvd S ☎ 702 698 7575, ⓦ cosmopolitanlasvegas. com. Stylish and contemporary, *The Cosmopolitan* is a great option at the heart of the Strip. The comfortable rooms come with colossal beds; even those that aren't suites have large living areas, while all except the cheapest have Strip-view balconies (a rarity in Las Vegas), and many overlook the Bellagio fountains. There's a spa plus top-quality restaurants and clubs,

Las Vegas's most luxurious spas

State-of-the-art spas in Las Vegas's top casinos pamper visitors with pools, steam rooms, fitness facilities and massage services. Daily entry normally costs around $50, and massages and other treatments from around $100 per half hour. Often, during busy periods, only guests staying in the relevant casino can use its spa. The following are the very best:

Aria	The Spa	Daily 5am–8pm	☎ 702 590 9600
Bellagio	Spa Bellagio	Daily 6am–8pm	☎ 702 693 7472
Caesars Palace	Qua	Daily 6am–8pm	☎ 866 782 0655
The Cosmopolitan	Sahra	Daily 7am–8pm	☎ 702 698 7171
Encore	Spa	Daily 7am–8pm	☎ 702 770 4772
Golden Nugget	Spa	Daily 7am–8pm	☎ 702 386 8186
Hard Rock	Reliquary	Daily 8am–7pm	☎ 702 693 5520
Mandalay Bay	Spa Mandalay	Daily 6am–8.30pm	☎ 877 632 7300
The Mirage	Spa	Daily 6am–7pm	☎ 702 791 7146
Planet Hollywood	Mandara	Daily 7am–7pm	☎ 702 785 5772
The Venetian	Canyon Ranch	Daily 6am–8pm	☎ 702 414 3600
Wynn	Spa	Daily 7am–8pm	☎ 702 770 3900

and the rooms aren't far from the lobby or the garage. **Resort fee $40/day. Mon–Thurs & Sun $200, Fri & Sat $320.**

THE CROMWELL MAP P.50, POCKET MAP G7. 3595 Las Vegas Blvd S ☎ 702 777 3777, ⓦ caesars.com/cromwell. Only in Las Vegas does having 188 rooms make you a "boutique hotel"; the Strip's smallest casino reopened in 2014 as an exclusive and expensive hideaway. **Resort fee $35/day. Mon–Thurs & Sun from $120, Fri & Sat $279.**

ENCORE MAP P.64, POCKET MAP J1. 3131 Las Vegas Blvd S ☎ 877 321 9966 or ☎ 702 770 7000, ⓦ wynnlasvegas.com. Las Vegas doesn't come any more luxurious than this; Encore truly is fit for a prince (just ask Harry Windsor). The huge, high-tech rooms are more subdued and earth-toned than the lurid reds the casino might lead you to expect, and all are suites, although the beds are screened off from the living areas rather than being separate rooms. **Resort fee $39/day. Mon–Thurs & Sun $229, Fri & Sat $339.**

EXCALIBUR MAP P.26, POCKET MAP B4. 3850 Las Vegas Blvd S ☎ 877 750 5464 or ☎ 702 597 7777, ⓦ excalibur.com. Cross the drawbridge, enter the Disneyesque castle, wheel your bag through the casino full of kids, ride the elevator to the top of the tower and amazingly enough, so long as you pay a little extra for one of the Royal Tower rooms, you've found yourself a nice place to stay. The older rooms are looking tired, though, and with its endless queues Excalibur itself can feel too big for comfort. **Resort fee $34/day. Mon–Thurs & Sun $38, Fri & Sat $150.**

FLAMINGO LAS VEGAS MAP P.50, POCKET MAP G6. 3555 Las Vegas Blvd S ☎ 888 902 9929 or ☎ 702 733 3111, ⓦ caesars.com/flamingo-las-vegas. So long as you stay at ground level, the *Flamingo* seems like a great hotel – light, airy and central, it's on a manageable scale, and has an attractive garden and pool, even live flamingoes. The rooms upstairs are very hit and miss, though, and can be grubby; only consider staying here if you find a truly exceptional rate. **Resort fee $35/day. Mon–Thurs & Sun $88, Fri & Sat $180.**

HARRAH'S MAP P.50, POCKET MAP G5. 3475 Las Vegas Blvd S ☎ 800 214 9110, ⓦ caesars.com/harrahs-las-vegas.

There's nothing to quicken the heart about Harrah's, the middle-of-the-Strip, middle-of-the-road casino that spent a couple of decades catering so assiduously to its long-standing customers that it was able to buy all its fancier neighbours. With that kind of success, they haven't felt compelled to change much. The standard rooms are rather ordinary, though there are some fancier suites. **Resort fee $35/day. Mon–Thurs & Sun $65, Fri & Sat $150.**

THE LINQ MAP P.50, POCKET MAP G5. 3535 Las Vegas Blvd S ☎ 800 634 6441, Ⓦ caesars.com/linq. The former Imperial Palace always ranked among the Strip's cheapest options; now renamed The Linq, it's maintaining that tradition by charging surprisingly low rates for such a central location. **Resort fee $35/day. Mon–Thurs & Sun $50, Fri & Sat $250.**

LUXOR MAP P.26, POCKET MAP B6. 3900 Las Vegas Blvd S ☎ 877 386 4658 or ☎ 702 262 4444, Ⓦ luxor.com. More than twenty years since this futuristic black-glass pyramid opened, it's sadly feeling its age. It can still be a thrill to stay in one of the original rooms, with their sloping windows, but there's a reason rooms in the newer tower next door cost a little more – they're in much better condition, and also have baths instead of just showers. **Resort fee $35/day. Mon–Thurs & Sun $57, Fri & Sat $156.**

MANDALAY BAY MAP P.26, POCKET MAP B7. 3950 Las Vegas Blvd S ☎ 877 632 7800 or ☎ 702 632 7777, Ⓦ mandalaybay. com. This far south of the central Strip, it makes sense to see Mandalay Bay as a self-contained resort. If you're happy to spend long days by its extravagant pool, and while away your evenings in its fine restaurants, bars, clubs and theatres, then it's well worth considering. The rooms are very comfortable, with both baths and walk-in showers. **Resort fee $37/day. Mon–Thurs & Sun $90, Fri & Sat $150.**

MGM GRAND MAP P.26, POCKET MAP C3. 3799 Las Vegas Blvd S ☎ 877 880 0880 or ☎ 702 891 7777, Ⓦ mgmgrand.com. While it may not be the world's largest hotel any more, the MGM Grand feels too big for its own good; once you've queued to check in and walked half a mile to your room, you may not feel up to venturing out to explore. Accommodation has been largely upgraded at the expense of its former character; the dark brown palette could be any convention hotel, anywhere. **Resort fee $37/day. Mon–Thurs & Sun $94, Fri & Sat $200.**

THE MIRAGE MAP P.64, POCKET MAP F4. 3400 Las Vegas Blvd S ☎ 800 374 9000 or ☎ 702 791 7444, Ⓦ mirage.com. The casino that gave Vegas a new definition of luxury seems like a fairly modest choice almost thirty years on, in that its rooms are smaller than the norm, and its bathrooms smaller still. They're still more than comfortable, though, with Strip and volcano views, and in a good location with excellent on-site amenities. **Resort fee $37/day. Mon–Thurs & Sun $169, Fri & Sat $250.**

NEW YORK–NEW YORK MAP P.26, POCKET MAP C3. 3790 Las Vegas Blvd S ☎ 866 815 4365 or ☎ 800 689 1797, Ⓦ newyorknewyork.com. Spending a night or two in Las Vegas's own Big Apple makes a more appealing prospect than a stay at most of its larger, less compact neighbours. Whether you opt for a "Park Avenue" or a slightly larger "Madison Avenue" room, the guest rooms are attractive and readily accessible, with some nice Art Deco touches, and the casino itself holds some excellent bars and restaurants. **Resort fee $37/day. Mon–Thurs & Sun $81, Fri & Sat $179.**

THE PALAZZO MAP P.64, POCKET MAP H3. 3325 Las Vegas Blvd S ☎ 866 263 3001 or ☎ 866 725 2990, Ⓦ palazzo.com. Staying at the Palazzo is fundamentally the same as staying at the Venetian (once you go downstairs, you're in the same building), but you'll find yourself slightly further from the heart of the action here. The actual rooms are very similar, with plush sleeping and living areas at slightly different levels, and huge marble bathrooms. **Resort fee $45/day. Mon–Thurs & Sun $215, Fri & Sat $299.**

PARIS MAP P.50, POCKET MAP G8. 3655 Las Vegas Blvd S ☎ 877 796 2096, caesars.com/paris-las-vegas. For many visitors, Paris represents an ideal compromise – you get to stay in an interesting big-name property, with excellent amenities plus "only in Vegas" features like the Eiffel Tower outside your window – without paying premium prices for opulent fittings you don't really need. The standard rooms are slightly faded now; for a little more pampering, opt for a newer "Red Room". Resort fee $37/day. Mon–Thurs & Sun $80, Fri & Sat $195.

PARK MGM MAP P.26, POCKET MAP C2. 3770 Las Vegas Blvd S ☎ 888 529 4828 or ☎ 702 730 7777, parkmgm.com. The long-standing but largely anonymous Monte Carlo underwent a major overhaul, and was split into two separate hotels – the 2700-room Park MGM and the pricier boutique NoMad (nomadlasvegas. com). Expect fancier rooms in brand new NoMad, more in keeping with the upscale CityCenter vibe. However, Park MGM rooms can be great value. **Resort fee $37/day. Mon–Thurs & Sun $69, Fri & Sat $199.**

PLANET HOLLYWOOD MAP P.50, POCKET MAP G9. 3667 Las Vegas Blvd S ☎ 866 919 7472, caesars.com/planet-hollywood. While Planet Hollywood's confusing layout can make it a long trek from your car to your room, once you're here it's a great-value central location. The rooms are in a style they call "Hollywood Hip", which tends to mean black and gold carpets and wallpaper; movie stills on the wall; and walk-in showers as well as baths. **Resort fee $37/day. Mon–Thurs & Sun $80, Fri & Sat $258.**

SLS LAS VEGAS MAP P.64, POCKET MAP L4. 2535 Las Vegas Blvd S ☎ 702 761 7000 or ☎ 888 696 2121, slslasvegas. com. Despite standing well north of the Strip proper, the former Sahara is thriving enough to charge substantial rates for its nicely refurbished rooms. **Resort fee $36/day. Mon–Thurs & Sun $100, Fri & Sat $230.**

THE STRATOSPHERE MAP P.64, POCKET MAP L2. 2000 Las Vegas Blvd S ☎ 702 380 7777, stratospherehotel.com. Much too far to walk to from either the

Strip or downtown, the Stratosphere is at least something of a destination in its own right – the rooms aren't in the 1000ft tower, but guests do get free admission. Find the right cut-price offer online, and its simple but sizeable rooms may suit your budget. **Resort fee $33/day. Mon–Thurs & Sun $46, Fri & Sat $155.**

TI (TREASURE ISLAND) MAP P.64, POCKET MAP G3. 3300 Las Vegas Blvd S ☎ 800 944 7444 or ☎ 702 894 7111, treasureisland.com. Like the building itself, the rooms at TI remain in good condition – they're nothing fancy, but they look reasonably fresh and have good beds – and the location is great too. These days, the whole place, and the pool in particular, attracts a young party crowd. Look out for online discounts. **Resort fee $37/day. Mon–Thurs & Sun $129, Fri & Sat $190.**

THE TROPICANA MAP P.26, POCKET MAP C4. 3801 Las Vegas Blvd S ☎ 888 381 8767 or ☎ 702 739 3626, troplv. com. Completely overhauled in 2010, this long-standing landmark can't quite match its Mirage-owned neighbours for dining and nightlife, but is a solid choice for a place to stay. It offers large, cream-and-orange rooms with new furnishings, an excellent pool complex and a location handy for the airport. **Resort fee $35/day. Mon–Thurs & Sun $100, Fri & Sat $200**

VDARA MAP P.40, POCKET MAP E9. 2600 W Harmon Ave ☎ 866 745 7767 or ☎ 702 590 2767, vdara.com. Hedonist holidaymakers might feel ill at ease with the austere steel-and-chrome aesthetic of this CityCenter all-suite hotel, and its lack of a casino, but if you're here to work, or just fancy an escape from Las Vegas's round-the-clock scene, it makes a peaceful and very comfortable retreat. **Resort fee $35/day. Mon–Thurs & Sun $119, Fri & Sat $250.**

THE VENETIAN MAP P.64, POCKET MAP G4. 3355 Las Vegas Blvd S ☎ 866 659 9643 or ☎ 702 414 1000, venetian.com. In terms of amenities in the property as a whole, and sheer comfort in its guest rooms, the Venetian ranks in the very top tier of Strip hotels; slightly more old-fashioned than Wynn, but still a true pampering experience. All the rooms are suites; you step down from the sleeping area, with its huge bed, to reach a sunken living space near the panoramic windows. Unusually, the price for advance bookings often remains the same for weekends as for weekdays. **Resort fee $45/day. Mon–Thurs & Sun $220, Fri & Sat $299.**

WYNN LAS VEGAS MAP P.64, POCKET MAP J2. 3131 Las Vegas Blvd S ☏ 877 321 9966 or ☏ 702 770 7000, ⓦ wynnlasvegas. com. With the arguable exception of the all-but-identical Encore alongside, this is as opulent as it gets in Vegas. The super-large rooms are tastefully decorated and equipped with luxurious linens, and bathrooms feature marble tubs, walk-in showers and even TVs. **Resort fee $39/day. Mon–Thurs & Sun $200, Fri & Sat $339.**

Downtown

THE D MAP P.80, POCKET MAP G12. 301 E Fremont St ☏ 702 388 2400, ⓦ thed.com. Since turning from Fitzgerald's into The D, this central downtown hotel has become a real bargain. All its rooms have had a top-to-bottom makeover (each has two queen beds) and the amenities downstairs are much improved. The one problem can be noise from the Experience outside. **Resort fee $22.50/day. Mon–Thurs & Sun $30, Fri & Sat $109.**

EL CORTEZ MAP P.80, POCKET MAP H12. 600 E Fremont St ☏ 800 634 6703 or ☏ 702 385 5200, ⓦ elcortezhotelcasino. com. Long renowned as Las Vegas's cheapest casino, El Cortez stands a short but, at night, potentially intimidating walk from the heart of Fremont Street. Once there, everything's in good shape, though the "Vintage" rooms, reached via the stairs, are no better than faded motel rooms. The "Cabana" suites, across the street, are much more appealing. Online packages for first-time guests offset room rates with free meals and gaming. **Resort fee $15/day. Mon–Thurs & Sun $37, Fri & Sat $99.**

FOUR QUEENS MAP P.80, POCKET MAP G12. 202 E Fremont St ☏ 800 634 6045 or ☏ 702 385 4011, ⓦ fourqueens. com. There's no real reason to pick this resolutely old-school downtown stalwart over any of its neighbours, though it has at least kept its rooms up to the adequate but unexciting level, say, of a $60-per-night national chain. **No resort fee. Mon–Thurs & Sun $45, Fri & Sat $109.**

FREMONT HOTEL MAP P.80, POCKET MAP G12. 200 E Fremont St ☏ 800 634 6460 or ☏ 702 385 3232, ⓦ fremontcasino.com. As one of the few downtown casinos owned by a major corporation – Boyd Gaming – the Fremont keeps its standards pretty high. The rooms are small but up to date, with pleasant decor and linens, and it's really not a bad alternative if you fancy being in the thick of the Fremont Street action. **Resort fee $15. Mon–Thurs & Sun $55, Fri & Sat $160.**

THE GOLDEN GATE MAP P.80, POCKET MAP G11. 1 E Fremont St ☏ 800 426 1906 or ☏ 702 385 1906, ⓦ goldengatecasino.com. Las Vegas's first ever hotel, one hundred years old in 2006, has been restyled as a 106-room "boutique hotel", with the promise that more suites will soon be added in a new extension. Yes, the rooms are small and the floors strangely lumpy, but you do get a true taste of Vegas history – plus, unfortunately, a blast of noise from the Experience. **Resort fee $22.50/day. Mon–Thurs & Sun $28, Fri & Sat $99.**

GOLDEN NUGGET MAP P.80, POCKET MAP G12. 129 E Fremont St ☏ 844 468 4438 or ☏ 702 385 7111, ⓦ goldennugget.com. Downtown's classiest option is the only hotel hereabouts with amenities – like its amazing pool – to match the Strip giants. The actual rooms, at their freshest but loudest in the Rush Tower overlooking Fremont Street, are smart and comfortable, if not all that exciting. **Resort fee $30/day. Mon–Thurs & Sun $49, Fri & Sat $124.**

LAS VEGAS HOSTEL MAP P.80, POCKET MAP J13. 1322 E Fremont St ☏ 800 550 8958 or ☏ 702 385 1150, ⓦ lasvegashostel.net. Popular with young travellers, this converted motel is almost a mile east of downtown in an area where walking is unadvisable. Adequate bare-bones accommodation includes four-, six-

and eight-bed single-sex and mixed dorms, and en-suite private rooms. There's also a pool, hot tub and organized activities. Wi-fi, parking and breakfast included. **Dorms $15–25/person; doubles $45.**

MAIN STREET STATION MAP P.80, POCKET MAP G11. 200 N Main St ☎ 800 465 0711 or ☎ 702 387 1896, ⓦ mainstreetcasino. com. A short but safe walk north of Fremont Street, this large and reasonably modern casino is always good value, for accommodation, food and drink; it's particularly good as an affordable base for a busy weekend. Ask for a room away from the interstate. **Resort fee $15. Mon–Thurs & Sun $40, Fri & Sat $100.**

THE PLAZA MAP P.80, POCKET MAP F11. 1 Main St ☎ 800 634 6575, ⓦ plazahotelcasino.com. The veteran Plaza, at the end of Fremont Street on the site of Las Vegas's original railroad station, pulled off a real coup in 2011. It bought up the brand-new fixtures and fittings from the prestigious Fontainebleu on the Strip, so badly hit by the recession it never even opened, and used them to turn its run-down rooms into some of the smartest and best-value lodgings around. **Resort fee $18/day. Mon–Thurs & Sun $45, Fri & Sat $110.**

The rest of the city

GOLD COAST MAP P.88, POCKET MAP G15. 4000 W Flamingo Rd, ☎ 888 402 6278 or ☎ 702 367 7111, ⓦ goldcoastcasino.com. Sedate, old-fashioned local casino, complete with bingo and a bowling alley, a hot half-mile west of the Strip (to which it's connected by free shuttle buses), but right by the fancier Rio and Palms. The rooms are not at all bad, but there's no earthly reason to stay unless the price is right. **Resort fee $21/day. Mon–Thurs & Sun $58, Fri & Sat $150.**

HARD ROCK HOTEL MAP P.88, POCKET MAP B16. 4455 Paradise Rd ☎ 800 473 7625, ⓦ hardrockhotel.com. If you know what you're coming for – to mix with partying 20-somethings – the *Hard Rock* will suit you perfectly. The rooms are cool and comfortable, and you can even open the floor-to-ceiling windows. It's too far from the Strip, though, to make a good base

for seeing the city as a whole. Weekends book up early; reserve in advance. **Resort fee $33/day. Mon–Thurs & Sun $70, Fri & Sat $279.**

ORLEANS MAP P.88, POCKET MAP A12. 4500 W Tropicana Ave ☎ 800 675 3267 or ☎ 702 365 7111, ⓦ orleanscasino. com. Provided you get one of its freshly renovated rooms and you have a car to get around, the Orleans, a mile west of the Strip, can serve as an affordable base to explore Las Vegas. The on-site cinema is a real boon. **Resort fee $21/day. Mon–Thurs & Sun $55, Fri & Sat $128.**

THE PALMS MAP P.88, POCKET MAP F16. 4321 W Flamingo Rd ☎ 866 942 7777 , ⓦ palms.com. One of the very few off-Strip casinos that you might genuinely want to stay in, rather than simply find a good-value rate for, the Palms is renowned for its clubs, gigs and weekend buzz. Things are much quieter on weekdays, but with such comfortable rooms and great pools, it can be a real bargain. **Resort fee $32/day. Mon–Thurs & Sun $99, Fri & Sat $169.**

RIO MAP P.88, POCKET MAP H15. 3700 W Flamingo Rd ☎ 866 746 7671, ⓦ caesars. com/rio-las-vegas. Part of the Caesars Entertainment empire, but separated by half a mile from its Strip siblings, the Rio really isn't a bad accommodation option. As well as high-class amenities and entertainment, it offers comfortable rooms (large but not suites, as they claim). The Palms is over the road, but you may feel you're missing out on all the action. **Resort fee $30/day. Mon–Thurs & Sun $85, Fri & Sat $149.**

SAM'S TOWN MAP P.88, POCKET MAP D12. 5111 Boulder Hwy ☎ 800 634 6371 or ☎ 702 456 7777, ⓦ samstownlv.com. Quietly prospering from meeting its middle-American customers' needs with Wild West shops, restaurants and bars, this old-fashioned locals casino stands resolutely apart from modern Las Vegas. If you want to dip into town but stay somewhere more peaceful, its comfortable rooms may suit you fine. It's a six-mile shuttle ride to the Strip so you're better off with a car. **Resort fee $20/day. Mon–Thurs & Sun $42, Fri & Sat $105.**

SUNSET STATION MAP P.88, POCKET MAP D13. 1301 W Sunset Rd, Henderson ☎ 702 547 7777, Ⓦ sunsetstation.sclv. com. This huge, attractive and well-equipped casino, ten miles southeast of the Strip en route towards Arizona, would seem impressive anywhere else. Here, despite its pool and fine restaurants, it counts as low-key, and only worth considering if the price is right or you're passing by. **Resort fee $20/day. Mon–Thurs & Sun $55, Fri & Sat $150.**

WESTGATE LAS VEGAS RESORT MAP P.88, POCKET MAP L5. 3000 Paradise Rd ☎ 888 796 3564, Ⓦ westgateresorts. com. How the mighty are fallen. The only reason to stay in the former Hilton – once, as home to Elvis, Las Vegas's premier hotel – is if you're attending a convention next door. Otherwise, the rooms just aren't good enough to compensate for the cut-off location and general air of decay. **Resort fee $34/day. Mon–Thurs & Sun $45, Fri & Sat $110.**

Mount Charleston

MOUNT CHARLESTON LODGE MAP P.98 Kyle Canyon Rd ☎ 702 872 5408, Ⓦ mtcharlestonlodge.com. Nineteen comfortably appointed log cabins, alongside the restaurant (see page 103) at the far end of Hwy-157. Lacking phones, wi-fi and TV reception, they're especially popular with honeymooners escaping Las Vegas. **$130.**

RETREAT ON CHARLESTON PEAK MAP P.98. 2 Kyle Canyon Rd ☎ 702 872 5500, Ⓦ retreatoncharlestonpeak.com. Set below Hwy-157, facing a towering rocky outcrop 17 miles up from US-95, the best accommodation option in the mountains holds 61 cosy, smart rooms, arranged around an artificial lake. **$77.**

Grand Canyon South Rim

BRIGHT ANGEL LODGE MAP P.98. Grand Canyon South Rim, AZ. Advance reservations ☎ 888 297 2757, Ⓦ grandcanyonlodges.com. Stretching along the South Rim and consisting of a grand lodge flanked by individual cabins, this fantastic-value option is usually booked up months in advance. Some units share bathrooms, while others enjoy canyon views. **Double with shared bathroom $100.**

EL TOVAR MAP P.98. Grand Canyon South Rim, AZ. Advance reservations ☎ 888 297 2757, Ⓦ grandcanyonlodges.com. At heart an overgrown log cabin, this magnificent, century-old hotel, a symphony in dark wood, is the definitive national park lodge. Although it's very close to the rim, only three of its 78 rooms offer substantial canyon views. Advanced booking necessary. **$220.**

Zion National Park

DESERT PEARL INN MAP P.98. 707 Zion Park Blvd, Springdale UT ☎ 435 772 8888, Ⓦ desertpearl.com. An absolutely gorgeous hotel, ranged alongside the Virgin River just outside the park, with superb views. From the parking areas it may look like a regular motel, but the actual rooms are huge, modern and very attractive, and there's a good pool with hot tubs. **$280.**

ZION LODGE MAP P.98. Zion National Park, UT. Advance reservations ☎ 888 297 2757 or ☎ 303 297 2757, same-day reservations ☎ 435 772 7700, Ⓦ zionlodge.com. The only accommodation option inside the national park, occupying pride of place on lush lawns in the heart of the Canyon. The forty en-suite cabins and six suites have gas fireplaces and private porches, while the 76 motel rooms are plainer, but still have porches or balconies. **Cabins $210, motel rooms $227.**

ESSENTIALS

The interior of Paris hotel and casino

Arrival

A very high proportion of visitors to Las Vegas **fly** into the city's only significant airport, not far east of the Strip, while all the rest **drive** across the empty desert from elsewhere in the USA. No passenger trains currently serve the city, though there's talk of constructing a high-speed link with Los Angeles.

By air

Las Vegas's ever-expanding **McCarran International Airport** (☎ 702 261 5211, ⊛ mccarran.com) lies immediately southeast of the Strip; aircraft pass within a mile of Mandalay Bay and the Tropicana as they taxi. However, both its terminals – confusingly numbered 1 and 3, since the new Terminal 3, used by all international flights, replaced the former Terminal 2 in 2012 – are accessed from the east, via Paradise Road. That means the closest Strip casinos are around three miles by road from the airport; the Venetian and Wynn more like five miles; and downtown hotels around seven miles.

Assuming you're not renting a car – in which case, note that all the rental companies are based at a separate, off-site facility (see page 118) – much the best way to transfer from the airport to your hotel is by **taxi**. In principle, a cab ride to the southern Strip (10–20min) will cost $16 and upwards, and to the northern Strip (20–30min) more like $30. If the traffic's bad you may have to pay up to $10 more.

Lone travellers may prefer to pay for a seat in a shared **Bell Trans shuttle bus** (☎ 800 274 7433, ⊛ bell-trans. com), which costs $7.50 to the Strip and $10 to downtown, but as these services drop off other passengers en route the journey time can be long, an hour or more for properties on the North Strip.

It is also possible, but even slower, to use the **RTC bus network** (see page 117), by taking route #109 from the airport to the South Strip Transfer Terminal, and changing there onto the Strip And Downtown Express, for a total fare of $6. The journey is likely to take at least half an hour for the South Strip, and over an hour for the North Strip and downtown.

Note that the **Las Vegas Monorail** (see page 118) does not serve the airport.

By car

The main driving route into Las Vegas is the **I-15** interstate, which connects the city with Los Angeles, 270 miles southwest, and Salt Lake City, 420 miles northeast. On Fridays especially, it tends to be clogged with cars arriving from southern California. Only if traffic is at a standstill is it worth leaving the interstate before you reach the exit closest to your final destination. If you're coming from California, therefore, you wouldn't normally expect to drive the full length of Las Vegas Boulevard, which runs parallel to I-15 from the southern end of the valley, and becomes the Strip roughly ten miles along.

Driving to Las Vegas from the Grand Canyon or anywhere else in Arizona, you'll approach the city along **US-93**, via the Hoover Dam. Follow the same road, which turns into Boulder Highway, all the way to downtown, or turn west, most likely on Tropicana Road or Flamingo Avenue, to reach the Strip.

By bus

Long-distance **Greyhound buses** (☎ 800 231 2222, ⊛ greyhound.com), which connect Las Vegas with other Southwestern cities including Los Angeles, Phoenix and Salt Lake City, stop downtown rather than on the Strip. The station is alongside the Plaza hotel, at 200 S Main Street.

Getting around

If you're visiting Las Vegas specifically to spend time on the Strip and/or downtown – as most visitors do – there's no point renting a car. Downtown is small enough to walk around, while a good **bus service** runs the length of the Strip and continues to downtown, and there are also several separate **monorail systems** on the Strip. Only if you expect to explore further afield – to outlying areas (see page 86), or to the surrounding desert (see page 96) – does a car become essential.

On foot

It comes as a big surprise to most visitors quite how much **walking** you have to do in Las Vegas. The Strip might look like a simple straight line on the map, but it has a peculiar geography all of its own; the colossal scale of the buildings tricks the eye, making them look smaller and nearer than they really are. Each individual casino can measure a mile end to end, while walking from, say, a restaurant in one property to a club in the next can take half an hour. Especially in summer, when the searing heat makes it all but impossible to walk more than a block or two outdoors, plotting a route from A to B becomes a real art, involving cutting through air-conditioned casinos, catching the occasional monorail and other such dodges.

By bus

While **RTC buses** (⊛ rtcsnv.com) cover the whole city, two routes meet almost all visitors' needs. Buy tickets before boarding; machines at stops along both routes sell passes for 2 hours ($6), 24 hours ($8) or 3 days ($20). All buses have wheelchair access.

The **Deuce on the Strip** (daily 24hr) runs the full length of the Strip, from Mandalay Bay to the Stratosphere, stopping outside all the casinos, and also loops around downtown, running north on Casino Center Boulevard and south on Las Vegas Boulevard. While its principal downtown stop is where the Fremont Street Experience meets Las Vegas Boulevard, it also stops in both directions at the Bonneville Transit Center (BTC), six blocks south at Bonneville and Casino Center, the main interchange for crosstown routes.

As the name suggests, the faster **Strip & Downtown Express**, or SDX, (daily 9am–midnight) also connects the Strip with downtown, but with fewer stops. In addition, rather than follow the Strip between Wynn Las Vegas and the Stratosphere, it detours west to run past the Convention Center. Downtown, the most useful stop is where the Fremont Street Experience meets Casino Center Boulevard, though the route loops back west beyond Fremont Street to terminate at the Las Vegas Premium Outlets (North) mall, and it also stops at the Bonneville Transit Center. Southbound SDX buses stop on the Strip outside the Fashion Show Mall, Bellagio, Excalibur and Mandalay Bay; northbound buses stop across from Mandalay Bay, and outside the MGM Grand, Paris and Wynn. The southern end of the route is the South Strip Transfer Terminal (SSTT), three miles southeast of Mandalay Bay at 6675 Gilespie Street, which connects with other bus routes and is also served by free airport shuttle buses.

In addition, various free **shuttle buses** connect the Strip with further-flung casinos. From Harrah's, buses run west to the Rio (every 30min, daily 10am–1am; ☎ 800 214 9110) and east to Sam's Town (every 1hr 30min, daily 9.30am–9.30pm; ☎ 800 897 8696). From the intersection of Flamingo Road with the Strip, buses run via the

Gold Coast to the Orleans (half-hourly departures, daily 9.30am–12.30am).

By monorail

Four separate monorail systems currently operate along different stretches of the Strip. The longest, but in some respects least useful, is the one officially called the **Las Vegas Monorail** (Mon 7am–midnight, Tues–Thurs 7am–2am, Fri–Sun 7am–3am; single trip $5, 1-day pass $13, 3-day pass $29; ⊚ lvmonorail.com). It runs behind the casinos on the eastern side of the Strip, from the MGM Grand to SLS Las Vegas, detouring east en route to call at the Convention Center. Had the route been extended south to the airport, and downtown in the north, it could have relieved Las Vegas's traffic problems. As it is, it's only conceivably helpful for hops along the southern Strip. Even then, all the stations are located right at the back of the relevant casinos, ten minutes' walk from their Strip entrances, so it can be slower to catch the Monorail than to walk.

All the other three monorail systems are **free**, and link small groups of neighbouring casinos. The southernmost connects Mandalay Bay with Excalibur, via Luxor. The second runs from the Monte Carlo, via Aria and Crystals in CityCenter, to Bellagio; it's a futuristic ride, but be warned that the Bellagio station is in that property's far southwestern corner, far from the casino floor and the Strip. Finally, there's the short link between the Mirage and TI now, which serves little practical function other than keeping pedestrians cool.

By car

Locals might find it hard to believe, but for visitors, **driving** in Las Vegas can be a real pleasure. The thrill of cruising along the Strip, with its sights and sounds and blazing signs,

only wears thin if you're actually trying to get somewhere by a certain time. Tourists tend naturally to avoid the worst times for traffic, like the morning rush hour.

Recently, however, the major Strip casinos have broken with tradition by imposing sizeable **parking fees** on all visitors, even their own overnight guests ("resort fees" do not include parking). Typically set at $8 for a short visit, $13/day for self-parking, and more like $20/day for valet parking, it's a major disincentive to renting a car. Most downtown casinos charge non-guests for parking, often waived if you use their restaurants or bars.

Car rental is available from almost every Strip or downtown hotel; as a rule each holds one or two outlets of the major rental chains. However, you can find a much wider choice, and usually better rates, if you pick up at the airport. That said, the major rental agencies are no longer based at the airport itself, but at the **McCarran Rent-A-Car Center**, three miles southwest at 7135 Gilespie Street, which is connected with the terminals by free shuttle buses. If you're already in the city and decide to rent a car, be sure to take a cab direct to the Rent-A-Car Center. Expect to pay around $40 per day, or $200 per week, for a compact car.

Campervans can be a comfortable way to move around, particularly if you are driving to the deserts. Campervan North America (☎ 208 712 8100, ⊚ campervannorthamerica.com) has a branch in Las Vegas at 4324 West Reno Avenue.

By taxi

Since Strip casinos started to charge parking fees, services such as Uber and Lyft have boomed in Las Vegas, and are readily available throughout the city. As for traditional **taxis**, you can't hail one on the street, but long lines of cabs wait at the airport, and at casino entrances. Meters calculate fares at $3.50 for the first mile and $2.76 for each additional mile, but also run if you're delayed in traffic, charging $1.08 every two minutes. There's an additional $2 surcharge for trips to or from the airport (see page 116). Fifteen percent is the usual tip for the driver.

Gambling

Gambling, or as they like to call it these days "**gaming**", lies at the root of everything in Las Vegas. Only one visitor in ten doesn't gamble at all; the rest lose an average of $500 each in the casinos. Whether you're pumping coins into a slot machine or trying to beat the dealer at blackjack, the rules always mean the casino enjoys the "house edge". So long as you're 21 or over, and carrying ID to prove it, you can gamble anywhere you like. The glamour of the large **Strip casinos** can be seductive, but the minimum stake for each game tends to be higher, and the odds a little worse. Many visitors prefer to gamble **downtown**, where the atmosphere is a bit more down-and-dirty and their money holds out longer. Either way, decide in advance how much you're prepared to lose, and stop if you reach that point.

In all casinos waitresses will ply you with free drinks as long as you are gambling; tips are expected. If you gamble for any length of time, join the casino's free players club; it can earn you meals, freebies and future stays.

Baccarat

Formerly the preserve of high-rolling "whales", **baccarat** (pronounced bah-kah-rah) accounts for over forty percent of the casinos' revenue from table games. Played with an ordinary pack in which each numbered card counts its face value (aces are 1 not 11), except tens, jacks, queens and kings, all valued at zero, it's a simple game of luck. Only two hands are dealt, the "player" and the "bank". Each aims to reach a total value of nine; you can bet on either, but the bank has a slightly better chance of winning. The house advantage comes because the casino rakes off a small commission.

Blackjack

Also known as "21" or "pontoon", **blackjack** remains Las Vegas's favourite card game. Players compete against the bank, attempting to build a hand that adds nearly, or exactly, to 21. Tens, jacks, queens and kings count as ten points, aces as either one or eleven. Players make their bets before receiving two cards, then each in turn plays their hand through to completion, saying "hit" to receive additional cards, and either "stand" to stop, or "bust" if the total exceeds 21. The dealer plays last, according to fixed rules that preclude individual judgement. The house advantage comes because players who go bust lose their stakes whether or not the dealer does too. Players can minimize that advantage by learning the "correct" response to every situation – it's so hard that some casinos happily provide gamblers with the relevant charts.

Craps

If you don't know how to play the dice game **craps**, played on a high-walled baize table, take a lesson (freely available in most casinos) – you'll never be able to learn it from watching. The basic idea is that a different "shooter" throws a pair of dice each time around. Players bet on either "pass" or "don't pass" before the first throw, known as the "come-out roll". If that throw is 7 or 11, "pass" has won; if it's 2, 3 or 12, "don't pass" wins. Anything else, and the shooter throws again, and keeps doing so until either matching the original throw – a win for "pass" – or throwing 7 – a win for "don't pass". All sorts of side bets capture the imaginations of serious gamblers.

Poker

In **poker**, players compete against each other, not the house, to build the best five-card hand (see page 120). The two most popular variations are Seven Card Stud, in which each player receives two cards face down, four face up, and then the last face down, and Texas Hold 'Em, in which your two face-down cards are supplemented by five face-up communal cards. The casino rakes off a percentage of each pot. You're therefore playing against whoever else happens to be around; it's possible to win, but it's a big risk to assume you're the best player at the table.

Casinos also offer what's effectively poker played in a **blackjack format**, in which each player attempts to beat the dealer. Formats include Let It Ride, Pai Gow Poker and Caribbean Stud.

Roulette

Roulette is the game in which a ball lands in a numbered slot in a rotating wheel. You can bet on the specific number, or group of numbers, and if the slot is "red" or "black". Winners are paid as though the wheel holds 36 slots, but it usually holds 38, thanks to two green slots, 0 and 00. Always look for wheels that hold only one zero slot, and thus offer better odds. You can't get your money back by repeatedly redoubling your stake; tables only allow bets up to a quickly reached maximum.

Slot machines

Casinos make more money from **slot machines** than from anything else. All machines are programmed to pay out a percentage of their intake as winnings. On average, visitors feed $1600 per day into every single machine in the city, and win $1500 back again, leaving the casino $100 profit. The slots downtown offer better odds than on the Strip.

A "non-progressive" machine always pays the same for a specific winning combination and pays smaller but more frequent jackpots. "Progressive" slots, such as Wheel of Fortune, are linked into networks where the overall jackpot can climb into millions of dollars, before someone scoops the lot.

Video poker is an addictive cross between traditional slot machines and the table game. The odds can be so good that on certain machines, players who play a perfect strategy have a slight advantage over the house.

Ranking of poker hands

Straight flush Five consecutive cards in the same suit.
Four of a kind Four aces, four sevens, etc.
Full house Three of a kind and a separate pair.
Flush Any five cards in the same suit.
Straight Five consecutive cards not in the same suit.
Three of a kind Three kings, three sixes, etc.
Two pair Two fours and two jacks, etc.
One pair Two tens, etc.

Sports betting

Las Vegas is all but unique in the USA in offering visitors the chance to bet on sports events legally, in the highly charged atmosphere of a major casino. Almost every casino has either a **Sports Book**, or if it covers horseracing as well, a Race and Sports Book, which vary from comfortable high-tech lounges to something more like a raucous neighbourhood sports bar. All offer much the same odds on any specific event and many offer "in-running" wagering, meaning moment-by-moment bets on games currently in progress.

Directory A–Z

Cinemas

Typical ticket prices for cinemas in Las Vegas are around $10 for matinee performances, starting before 6pm, and $15 for evening shows.
AMC Town Square 18 Town Square, 6587 Las Vegas Blvd S ☎702 362 7283, ⓦamctheatres.com.
Brenden Theatres & IMAX The Palms, 4321 W Flamingo Rd ☎702 507 4849, ⓦbrendentheatres.com.
Century 18 Orleans, 4500 W Tropicana Ave ☎702 889 1220, ⓦcinemark.com.
Century 18 Sam's Town, 5111 Boulder Hwy ☎702 547 1732, ⓦcinemark.com.
Regal 13 Sunset Station, 1301 W Sunset Rd, Henderson ☎844 462 7342, ⓦregmovies.com.
There is no cinema on the Strip.

Crime

While you're safe in the major public spaces of Las Vegas, such as inside the security-conscious casinos, crime can be a problem elsewhere. Away from the crowded Strip, which has its own problems with **pickpockets** and bag-snatchers, you can feel exposed and vulnerable if you walk any distance outdoors. It's essential to keep your cash hidden at all times, not to flaunt valuables like cameras and iPads, and not to tell strangers your hotel room number. Be cautious in multistorey parking garages, especially at night, and try to park close to the exits. In times when mass shootings can happen anywhere in the US, be aware of any suspicious situations.

Electricity

The **electricity** supply in Las Vegas, as in all of the USA, is 110 volts AC, and uses two-pin plugs. Bring or buy an adapter, and if necessary a voltage converter as well, if you're travelling from a country that uses a different system and need to use your own electrical appliances.

Health

In any medical emergency, call ☎911. The front desk or phone operator at your hotel will be able to advise on sources of appropriate help. **Hospitals** that have 24hr emergency rooms include Sunrise Hospital, 3186 S Maryland Parkway (☎702 961 5000, ⓦsunrisehospital.com), and the University Medical Center, 1800 W Charleston Blvd (☎702 383 2000, ⓦumcsn.com). For more minor issues, head to the Harmon Medical Center, 150 E Harmon Ave (Mon–Fri 8am–8pm; ☎702 796 1116).

Emergency numbers

In any medical or security emergency, call ☎911.

Twenty-four-hour **pharmacies** on the Strip include the CVS Pharmacy, alongside the Monte Carlo at 3758 Las Vegas Blvd S (📞 702 262 9028) and Walgreens, beside the main Palazzo entrance at 3339 Las Vegas Blvd S (📞 702 369 8166).

To find a local **dentist**, contact the Nevada Dental Association (📞 702 255 4211, 🌐 nvda.org).

Internet

Every casino/hotel in Las Vegas provides in-room **wi-fi** access for its guests, but only rarely is it free. In almost all cases, internet access forms the largest component of the compulsory "resort fee" (see page 107), which typically costs at least $20 per day, and may well cover one device only; elsewhere, hotel guests can generally choose to pay a stand-alone fee of around $15 per day. On top of that, if you're spending time in a casino other than one you're staying in, you won't normally have wi-fi access.

Several casinos, however, including most of the MGM Resorts properties, offer **free wi-fi** access to everyone in their public areas, as opposed to the guest rooms. In addition, a handful of shops and cafés along the Strip provide free wi-fi to customers (and anyone who happens to be in the immediate vicinity): *Coffee Bean & Tea Leaf* in Planet Hollywood's Miracle Mile (see page 56); and the Apple Store and *Starbucks* in the Fashion Show Mall (see page 70).

Free wi-fi is also available throughout McCarran International Airport.

Las Vegas Power Pass

Las Vegas Power Pass (📞 702 685 6578, 🌐 lasvegaspass.com) is the sightseeing card which gives holders entry to over 50 top Vegas attractions, bus tours and museums. The pass is available for 1 day ($89), 2 days ($125), 3 days ($170) or 5 days ($251).

LGBTQ travellers

Although Las Vegas, or at least the parts of the city that visitors are at all likely to see, is **gay-friendly**, the casinos make little show of catering to gay travellers in any specific sense. No Strip casino currently holds a specifically gay club, so the city's gay-oriented nightlife focuses instead around what's fondly known as the "**Fruit Loop**", a mile east of the Strip, where Paradise Road, running south from the Hard Rock, meets Naples Drive. Well-known clubs in the neighbourhood include Piranha (see page 95), but there are none exclusively geared towards women.

The best source of information on current issues and events in Las Vegas's gay community are 🌐 gaylasvegas.com, 🌐 gogaynevada.com or 🌐 lasvegaspride.org.

Since same-sex marriage was declared legal in Nevada in 2014, the major casino chapels have rushed to offer gay wedding ceremonies, even if certain private chapels have refused. The **Gay Chapel of Las Vegas**, 1205 Las Vegas Blvd S (📞 702 384 0771, 🌐 gaychapeloflasvegas.com) offers a full range of ceremonies; Elvis is optional.

The annual **Las Vegas Pride** event, celebrated in late October (📞 866 930 3336, 🌐 lasvegaspride.org), kicks off with a Friday night parade through downtown, while the Saturday sees an open-air festival in Sunset Park, at the corner of Sunset Road and Eastern Avenue, 10 miles south of downtown.

In May, the **Nevada Gay Rodeo Association** (🌐 ngra.com) holds the three-day BigHorn Rodeo at Horseman's Park, 5800 E Flamingo Rd.

Money

Las Vegas is not a budget destination in any meaningful sense. The days are gone when casinos used cut-price food and entertainment to lure in gamblers. Now everything from restaurants to showrooms have to make a profit, and prices are high. A typical all-you-can-eat buffet costs $20 or more for dinner; a run-of-the-mill restaurant more like $40 per head, without drinks; and a gourmet place double that or more. Tickets for a show can easily cost $100 or more, while a night out in a big club is liable to cost hundreds, and potentially thousands, of dollars. Hotel room rates are generally good value, and on weekdays compare favourably with what you'd get for the same money elsewhere in the USA, but can run into hundreds per night on weekends. On top of that, of course, the average visitor also loses several hundred dollars gambling.

As for how you bring your money, it's assumed everywhere that you'll use a **credit card** for all significant expenses. It's extremely easy to get cash anywhere on the Strip; ATMs are everywhere, though all tend to charge around $3 for withdrawals.

Travellers from overseas are advised not to bring foreign cash; there are no banks on the Strip, and while the casinos will gladly change your cash you won't get a good rate. Dollar **travellers' cheques** are accepted as cash everywhere, though few visitors bring them these days.

Phones

Foreign visitors can assume that their **mobile phones** (cell phones) will work in Las Vegas, though it's worth checking with your phone provider that your existing payment scheme will cover you there, and what the call charges are. Many providers offer short-term pricing packages designed to make holiday phone usage more affordable. If you plan to access the internet using your phone, make sure that you know your provider's roaming charges, which may well be extremely expensive.

For all calls, you can make tremendous savings by using **Skype**, or similar programmes, to make free wi-fi calls from your phone or laptop. Alternatively, prepaid **phone cards** are widely available from casino convenience stores, petrol (gas) stations, supermarkets and other outlets. Many casinos, especially those that charge resort fees (see page 107), offer guests free local phone calls; making an international call from your hotel room phone is always liable to be very expensive.

Smoking

Smoking remains legal in the public areas of all casinos, and in bars that do not serve food. It is forbidden in restaurants, including those inside casinos, though smoke does waft into those restaurants that are open to

Public holidays

Jan 1 New Year's Day
Jan 15 Martin Luther King Jr's Birthday
3rd Mon in Feb Presidents' Day
Last Mon in May Memorial Day
July 4 Independence Day
1st Mon in Sept Labor Day
2nd Mon in Oct Columbus Day
Nov 11 Veterans' Day
Last Thurs in Nov Thanksgiving Day
Dec 25 Christmas Day

the casino floor. All hotels offer non-smoking rooms.

Tax

Sales tax of 8.25 percent is charged on all purchases in Las Vegas. Hotel rates are subject to an additional **room tax** of twelve percent on the Strip, and thirteen percent downtown (see page 107).

Time

Las Vegas is in the **Pacific Time Zone**, three hours behind the Eastern Time Zone. It's almost always eight hours behind the UK, though clocks in the US move forward by one hour on the second Sunday in March and back one hour on the first Sunday in November, placing them briefly out of synch with clocks in the UK.

Tipping

Tipping etiquette is not as complicated as many visitors imagine; if you find yourself wondering whether to tip, do. Servers in restaurants depend on tips for their income, and expect at least fifteen percent. So do cab drivers. If someone carries your bags, tip $1–2 per bag; valet parking attendants expect $2; and it's usual to leave a tip of $1 or $2 per day when you leave your hotel room. When gambling, it's considered appropriate to tip the dealer a chip or two if you win. Bar staff, or casino waitresses bringing free drinks, expect $1–2 per drink.

Tourist information

The best single source of information on the city is ⓦ lasvegas.com, the website of the **Las Vegas Convention and Visitor Authority** (LVCVA). They also run a visitor centre at 3150 Paradise Rd, half a mile east of the Strip (Mon–Fri 8am–5pm; ☏ 877 847 4858), but it offers nothing you can't find much more easily elsewhere.

Other useful websites include:
ⓦ **dmckee.lvablog.com** The "Stiffs

and Georges" blog is a lively but serious source of news and comment on Las Vegas and the casino industry.
ⓦ **eatinglv.com** This long-running blog holds a huge archive of restaurant reviews.
ⓦ **everythinglv.com** Weekly online updates on the latest Las Vegas news, plus reader forums.
ⓦ **lasvegassun.com** Las Vegas's best daily newspaper website.
ⓦ **lasvegasweekly.com** A good source of current listings, plus a handy archive of their annual "Best of Las Vegas" awards in all sorts of categories.
ⓦ **lvol.com** Schedules, reservations and reviews for concerts and shows; a good place to find out what's happening while you're in town.

Travellers with disabilities

The **Las Vegas Convention and Visitors Authority** offers detailed advice for disabled visitors; download the Access Las Vegas brochure from ⓦ lasvegas.com, or call their advice line on ☏ 702 892 0711.

All the casinos in Las Vegas are **wheelchair accessible** and offer hotel rooms designed to suit visitors with disabilities. Don't underestimate the sheer scale of each casino, let alone the Strip as a whole; an individual destination like a restaurant or a theatre may be a long way from the nearest parking space. If you need to rent specific mobility equipment, contact Ability Center, 6001 S Decatur Blvd (☏ 702 434 3030, ⓦ abilitycenter. com). For public transport, both Bell Trans shuttle buses from the airport (☏ 800 274 7433, ⓦ airportshuttlelasvegas.com) and RTC buses in the city itself (ⓦ rtcsnv.com) are wheelchair accessible. If you plan to drive yourself, note that the national rental chains offer adapted vehicles, and visitors can arrange temporary free **disabled parking permits** via the

Nevada Department of Motor Vehicles (☎ 775 684 4750 or ☎ 702 486 4368, ⊛ dmvnv.com).

Tours

Las Vegas does not offer the kind of **sightseeing tours** familiar in other cities. Almost everything of interest in the city itself is in and around the casinos; you can't really appreciate them from a passing bus, and they're too big to explore more than one or two at a time on foot. **Bus tours** do, however, head further afield. Thus Gray Line (☎ 702 739 7777, ⊛ graylinelasvegas.com) offers tours to the Hoover Dam (4hr 30min; $72); the Grand Canyon West Rim (11hr; $240); and the Grand Canyon South Rim (14hr; $180). You can also get lucky and buy these tours for much less. Helicopter operators, including Maverick (☎ 702 261 0007, ⊛ maverickhelicopter. com) and Sundance (☎ 702 736 0606, ⊛ sundancehelicopters.com), offer brief day or night **"flightseeing" tours** over the Strip, at typical prices from $84 for a flight lasting less than fifteen minutes. They and other companies also fly day-trippers east to the Grand Canyon (see page 101).

For something totally different with an extra shot of adrenaline, try RZR Zero 1 Tours. They provide access to Nevada's diverse terrain and new trails by putting you behind the wheel of a high-performance dune buggy. From $224. (☎ 702 361 9100 6975, ⊛ zero1.vegas), Speedway Blvd. D-105, Las Vegas).

Travelling with children

In the early 1990s, Las Vegas flirted briefly with the idea that it might become a child-friendly destination to match Orlando, Florida. That dream was swiftly abandoned; gambling and kids don't make a good mix. Even so, many visitors bring their **kids** to the city; the Strip sidewalk is thronged until after midnight with parents pushing cumbersome buggies and struggling with exhausted children.

There's still a lot about Las Vegas that will appeal to kids, from the castles and pyramids, volcanoes and fountains on the Strip, to more specific paying attractions. Among the most popular with children are the Secret Garden and Dolphin Habitat at the Mirage; Shark Reef at Mandalay Bay; the Bodies and Titanic exhibitions at Luxor; the gondolas at the Venetian; CSI: The Experience at the MGM Grand; and the roller coasters and thrill rides at New York–New York, Circus Circus and the Stratosphere.

All the casinos welcome children as guests. Strictly speaking, **under-21s** are not allowed in gambling areas, which means that family groups have to keep walking rather than linger on the casino floor. Casinos do not offer babysitting services, but can provide details of babysitting agencies.

Note that in many casinos, some or all of the swimming pools now operate as adults-only "dayclubs", with drinking, dancing and partying; it's worth checking in advance before you go ahead and book your accommodation.

Weddings

Thanks to Nevada's notoriously minimal legal requirements, and especially the lack of an obligatory waiting period, around 120,000 people get married in Las Vegas each year.

At its simplest, arranging a Vegas wedding is very straightforward. First of all, you need a **Nevada marriage licence**. To get that, both parties must appear in person at the Clark County Marriage License Bureau, 200 South Third St (Mon–Thurs 8am–midnight, Fri–Sun 12pm–midnight; ☎ 702 455 4416, ⊛ clarkcountynv.gov). So long as both are aged 18 or over, not married already and can show picture ID, they'll sell you a licence for $77 (credit cards $82, debit cards not accepted). Note that there isn't an office on the Strip.

If you've made an advance reservation, you can then walk with your licence to the office of the **Commissioner of Civil Marriages**, on the sixth floor at 330 S Third St (Mon–Thurs 2–6pm, Fri 9.30am–8.45pm, Sat 12.30–8.45pm, Sun 9am–5pm; ☏ 702 671 0577, ⓦ clarkcountynv.gov) and pay another $75 cash to have the actual ceremony performed. One witness is required; ideally you should bring your own, though what the Commissioner charmingly calls "unsavoury individuals" lurk outside the offices, hoping to sell their services as witnesses.

Just because it's possible to have a quick, cheap wedding in Las Vegas, however, doesn't mean that's what most couples actually do. Instead, most marriages are celebrated in wedding chapels, which can be stand-alone structures of the kind reviewed throughout this book or yet another component in the huge casino-hotels. You can find full listings of chapels and wedding planners on the official Las Vegas CVB website, ⓦ lasvegas. com, and also on the casinos' own websites.

Prices at **wedding chapels** range upwards from around $200 all-in for a bare-bones ceremony. For the full works, which in Las Vegas can include helicopter flights to the Grand Canyon or pretty much anything else you care to mention, the bill can of course run into thousands of dollars. The biggest hidden expense is likely to be photography; be sure to check whether you or your guests will be allowed to bring cameras, and if not, how much the official photos or footage will cost.

Finally, note that now **gay marriage** has become legal in Nevada all the major casino chapels, and most but not all of the private chapels, are happy to perform gay weddings. For more details, see page 122.

Festivals and events

Compared to other American cities, Las Vegas does not have an extensive calendar of annual events. In terms of attracting crowds, the biggest events tend to be the opening of new casinos and, even more exciting, the implosions of old ones.

NASCAR Weekend

Early March ⓦ lvms.com
Three days of racing at the Las Vegas Motor Speedway, 7000 Las Vegas Blvd N at Speedway Blvd.

St Patrick's Day

March 17
Pubs, clubs, casinos and restaurants all celebrate St Patrick's Day.

World Series of Poker

Late May to mid-July ⓦ poker. wsop.com
The world's premier poker tournament has been held at the Rio since 1995.

Las Vegas Helldorado Days

Mid-May ⓦ elkshelldorado.com
Five nights of pro rodeo action in Symphony Park – at 100 S Grand Central Parkway, alongside downtown's Smith Center – plus a Saturday night parade downtown.

National Finals Rodeo

Early Dec ⓦ nfrexperience.com

Conventions and trade shows

When planning a visit, it's useful to know when the city's biggest **conventions** are happening as room rates can soar.
Mid-Jan Consumer Electronics Show
Mid-Feb Men's Apparel Guild (MAGIC) convention
Early April National Association of Broadcasters convention
Mid-Aug Men's Apparel Guild (MAGIC) convention (again)
Early Nov Specialty Equipment Manufacturers Association (SEMA) convention

Ten-day pro rodeo event at the Thomas & Mack Center, 4505 S Maryland Parkway.

New Year's Eve

December 31
The biggest night in the city's calendar, marked by concerts and festivities.

Chronology

1598 Spain claims what's now southern Nevada as part of the colony of New Mexico.

1829 Mexican explorers name an unexpected oasis of grasslands "Las Vegas" – "The Meadows".

1847 USA acquires New Mexico.

1864 Nevada becomes a state.

1905 The railroad arrives. Las Vegas is established on May 15, when forty newly drawn blocks are auctioned.

1909 Nevada becomes the first US state to outlaw gambling.

1931 Nevada marks the end of Prohibition by legalizing gambling – the only state to do so.

1935 Hoover Dam completed. Las Vegas hosts first convention.

1938 Guy McAfee, former chief of LA's vice squad, takes over the Pair-O-Dice Club, on what he dubs "The Strip".

1940 Las Vegas's population reaches eight thousand.

1941 El Rancho opens as the Strip's first fully fledged resort.

1946 Mobster "Bugsy" Siegel opens the Flamingo; he's murdered six months later after heavy losses.

1950s An unstoppable flow of new Strip resorts includes the Desert Inn, the Sands, the Riviera, the Dunes and the Hacienda. Desert A-bomb tests can be seen and heard from the city.

1966 Caesars Palace, the first themed casino, opens. Howard Hughes is asked to leave the Desert Inn because he isn't gambling; instead, he buys it, along with the Sands, the Silver Slipper and the New Frontier, marking the end of Mob domination.

1969 Kirk Kerkorian opens the world's largest hotel – the Las Vegas Hilton – which hosts Elvis's rebirth as a karate-kicking lounge lizard.

1973 Kirk Kerkorian again opens the world's largest hotel – the original MGM Grand, now Bally's. Steve Wynn takes over downtown's Golden Nugget.

1983 Following disastrous fires at the MGM Grand and the Hilton, Las Vegas seems about to be eclipsed by Atlantic City; direct flights between New York and Las Vegas are discontinued.

1989 Steve Wynn opens the opulent Mirage, complete with volcano. Benny Binion dies, with his Horseshoe downtown still Las Vegas's most profitable casino.

1993 In a short-lived bid to reinvent Las Vegas as a child-friendly destination, Luxor, Treasure Island and the new MGM Grand all open.

1995 Downtown roofed over to create Fremont Street Experience.

1997 New York–New York opens; in a craze for building replica cities, it's followed by Bellagio in 1998 and the Venetian and Paris in 1999.

2005 Harrah's buys Caesars Entertainment, leaving the Strip largely owned by two huge corporations. Wynn Las Vegas opens.

2009 Despite recession, MGM Mirage completes CityCenter.

2011 Carolyn Goodman succeeds her husband Oscar as mayor.

2014 Las Vegas High Roller opens.

2015 Caesars Entertainment goes into bankruptcy; emerges in 2016.

2016 Venetian owner Sheldon Adelson is major donor to Donald Trump's presidential campaign.

2017 A gunman opens fire at a crowd of concert-goers on the Strip, killing 58 and injuring more than 500 people.

Publishing Information
Fourth Edition 2019

Distribution
UK, Ireland and Europe
Apa Publications (UK) Ltd; sales@roughguides.com
United States and Canada
Ingram Publisher Services; ips@ingramcontent.com
Australia and New Zealand
Woodslane; info@woodslane.com.au
Southeast Asia
Apa Publications (SN) Pte; sales@roughguides.com
Worldwide
Apa Publications (UK) Ltd; sales@roughguides.com
Special Sales, Content Licensing and CoPublishing
Rough Guides can be purchased in bulk quantities at discounted prices. We can
create special editions, personalised jackets and corporate imprints tailored to
your needs. sales@roughguides.com.
roughguides.com
Printed in China by RR Donnelley Asia Printing Solutions Limited
All rights reserved
© 2019 Apa Digital (CH) AG
License edition © Apa Publications Ltd UK

A catalogue record for this book is available from the British Library
The publishers and authors have done their best to ensure the accuracy and
currency of all the information in **Pocket Rough Guide Las Vegas**, however, they
can accept no responsibility for any loss, injury, or inconvenience sustained by
any traveller as a result of information or advice contained in the guide.

Rough Guide Credits
Author: Greg Ward
Updater: Wesołych Świąt
Editor: Siobhan Warwicker
Cartography: Katie Bennett
Managing editor: Rachel Lawrence
Picture editor: Michelle Bhatia

Cover photo research: Tom Smyth
Original design: Richard Czapnik
Senior DTP coordinator: Dan May
Head of DTP and Pre-Press:
Rebeka Davies

Help us update

We've gone to a lot of effort to ensure that this edition of the **Pocket Rough Guide Las Vegas** is accurate and up-to-date. However, things change – places get "discovered", opening hours are notoriously fickle, restaurants and rooms raise prices or lower standards. If you feel we've got it wrong or left something out, we'd like to know, and if you can remember the address, the price, the hours, the phone number, so much the better.

Please send your comments with the subject line "**Pocket Rough Guide Las Vegas Update**" to mail@uk.roughguides.com. We'll credit all contributions and send a copy of the next edition (or any other Rough Guide if you prefer) for the very best emails.

Photo Credits

(Key: T-top; C-centre; B-bottom; L-left; R-right)

Alamy 12B, 23, 28, 38, 61, 75, 87, 92, 98

Denise Truscello/Caesars Entertainment 51

Erik Kabik 60

iStock 6, 77, 85

MGM Resorts International 2TL, 13B, 16L, 17T, 18C, 19C, 33, 36, 104/105

Shutterstock 1, 2BL, 2MC, 2BC, 4, 10, 11B, 12T, 14T, 15T, 15B, 16R, 17B, 18T, 18C, 19T, 20T, 20C, 20B, 21T, 21C, 21B, 25, 30, 37, 39, 41, 42, 45, 49, 53, 55, 56, 59, 81, 90, 97, 100, 102, 103, 114/115

The Boulevard 91

Tim Draper/Rough Guides 11T, 13C, 14B, 19C, 27, 31, 34, 46, 54, 63, 66, 68, 71, 72, 79, 82, 83, 84, 86, 89, 94, 95

Cover: Stratosphere Tower and Holiday Motel, Las Vegas Strip **Susanne Kremer/4Corners Images**

Index

NOTES

ROUGH GUIDES

ESCAPE THE EVERYDAY

ADVENTURE BECKONS
YOU JUST NEED TO KNOW WHERE TO LOOK

31192021700255